Language Development in Children with Special Needs

with Special Needs

Performative Communication

Language Development in Children with Special Needs

Performative Communication

Iréne Johansson

translated into English and adapted by Eva Thomas

Jessica Kingsley Publishers
London and Philadelphia

First published as *Språkutveckling hos handikappade barn* by
Studentlitteratur
PO Box 141
S-221 00 Lund, Sweden
First English language edition published in the United Kingdom in 1994 by
Jessica Kingsley Publishers Ltd
116 Pentonville Road
London N1 9JB, England
and
325 Chestnut Street,
Philadelphia, PA19106, USA

Second Impression 1999

Library of Congress Cataloging in Publication Data
Johansson, Iréne, 1947–
[Språkutveckling hos handikappade barn. English]
Language development in children with special needs : performative
communication / Iréne Johansson : translated into English and adapted by Eva Thomas.
p. cm. Includes bibliographical references and index.
ISBN 1-85302-241-1 (pbk.)
1. Language disorders in children—Treatment. 2. Language
acquisition—Parent participation. [. Title.
RJ496.L35J6313 1994
618.92'85506—dc20

British Library Cataloguing in Publication Data
Johansson, Iréne
Language Development in Children with
Special Needs:Performaive Communication
I. Title II. Thomas, Eva
371.9

ISBN 1085302-241-1

Printed and Bound in Great Britain by
Athenaeum Press, Gateshead, Tyne and Wear

Contents

Preface

This book was translated and adapted from the Swedish text *Språkutveck-ling hos handikappade barn*, by Iréne Johansson. The intervention method it describes has been used with great success in Sweden but until now the method has not been available in English.

Expert advice on adapting the sound stimulation and phonological content of the method to British clinical settings was kindly given by Professor Grunwell, Department of Speech Pathology, De Montfort University. Mavis Meredith, Superintendent Paediatric Physiotherapist, advised on gross and fine motor stimulation. Useful advice and feedback was also obtained from Speech and Language Therapists who used the first version of the English text.

The use of signs was translated from the Swedish Sign Language to the British Sign Language.

A research study has been carried out to assess the effectiveness of the translated and adapted method on British Down's Syndrome children. This comprised an evaluation of the treatment method on a British sample of Down's Syndrome children from 0 to 18 months of age, with identical research design to that used in the Swedish study reported in this book.

In order to carry out a study in Britain, Speech and Language Therapists had to be found who would supply subjects for the experimental and the control groups from their own caseload. This was the way Johansson had recruited her experimental group.

Therapists were invited to attend workshops to receive training in the application of the intervention method.

Data were collected for 17 subjects; this is similar to the number in the original Swedish study, the findings of which were based on data from 17–20 subjects.

A full presentation of the results of the study are given in a report (Thomas, 1994) prepared for the Primary Care Development Fund

(South East Thames Regional Health Authority), who funded the British study. A summary of the findings is given below.

The study observed when four important communicative skills emerged in children using the method described in this book. The four skills observed were: baby turning towards a human voice, reduplicated babbling (for example, 'bababa'), performative communication, and single words. It should be noted that the observations do not provide information about qualitative or quantitative aspects of development. The observations should also be viewed in general rather than specific terms, since they were collected by the parents in collaboration with the children's Speech and Language Therapist.

The figures below show the mean age at which the various communication skills emerged in the project children, compared with the corresponding data from Johansson. It should be noted that Johansson only published median values; therefore median values are shown for those data.

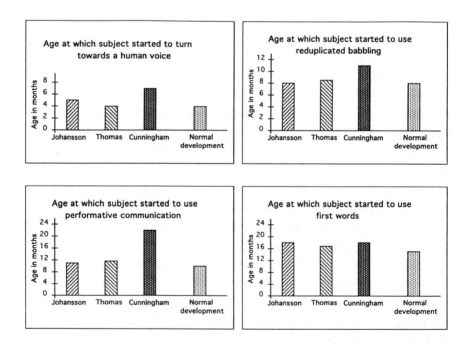

In the absence of data from a control group, published values for British Down's Syndrome children (Cunningham, 1982) are shown in these figures. Cunningham's data are based on observations of more than 150

babies with Down's syndrome whose parents had received some help and guidance on how to stimulate them. Children with severe complications, whose developmental milestones were very late indeed, were excluded from Cunningham's study. Only children with profound bilateral hearing impairment were excluded from the groups using the method described in this book. Since the children using this method were selected at such an early age, often at about one month, very little was known about the severity of the developmental delay. Therefore the Speech and Language Therapists contributing subjects would not have been able to select children in a certain ability range.

Data corresponding to normal development (Capute *et al.,* 1981; Bates *et al.,* 1977) are also shown for comparison.

From the figures it will be seen that the values obtained in the study of British children using the method presented here (Thomas, 1994) are very similar to those obtained by Johansson in the Swedish study. This indicates that the Johansson method has worked as well for the British group regarding the development of the communication skills considered.

Both children and their parents seem to benefit from the programmes, support and advice given by the Speech and Language Therapists even when the child is an infant less than three months old. By the overwhelmingly positive comments from the parents it is felt that the early intervention has helped the parent–child relationship by increased parental communication awareness, more appropriate expectations of the child's progress and an improvement in the children's communication skills during the first few years of life.

Early language intervention is effective, particularly in developing alternative communication methods before the first words appear. The children are able to develop symbolic capacity by using specific gestures and signs before they are able to use words.

As a group, the children of this study became more efficient communicators at an earlier age than is expected in Down's syndrome.

Eva Thomas
July 1994

PART ONE

Theoretical Background to Early Language Intervention

Introduction

This book is based on experiences from the research project *Early Language Intervention in Children with Down's Syndrome*. The project ran from 1981 to 1986. During that period a total of 56 children took part.

The development of the methodology and material for language intervention in young children with learning disability is based on current theories of speech, language and communication acquisition. The research project was a joint collaboration with Specialist Speech and Language Therapists in Stockholm County and Specialist Preschool Teachers in Värmland County, Sweden.

Our intervention method is based on a theoretical model of speech, language and communication development in which the child's participation during the learning process is seen as fundamental. In all suggested intervention activities the child should take an active part and he/she is never seen as a passive recipient. The child and the parent carry out the activities together if the child is not able to carry the activity out on his/her own.

The child's development, both in general terms and more specifically speech and communication development, is believed to depend on an interaction between innate prerequisites and environmental factors. The innate prerequisites determine which properties and events in the environment the child can perceive and process, whilst at the same time influences from the environment are believed to be necessary for the innate prerequisites to develop.

Initially, the inner prerequisites are limited to functions which are innate. By stimulation and influences from the surrounding world the innate functions change and develop, provided there are suitable properties in the stimulation to which the child is exposed. Experiences are perceived and processed in a manner which changes as a result of learning and development. This spiral-like interaction between inner abilities and environmental stimulation make the child capable of perceiving even more complex information about the world.

This theoretical description of child development is assumed to cover all children's development regardless of whether learning disability is present or not. All children are different from each other. An adult who uses our intervention method therefore needs considerable knowledge and understanding to judge the susceptibility of the inner abilities and the type of stimulation chosen in order to create the developmentally most beneficial situation for the child.

A child with learning disability has reduced functions in one way or another in respect of the innate abilities. It is more important for these types of children that the stimulation is adapted to suit each individual child. It is also important to take into account that some types of reduced function can and should be compensated by technical aids and alternative communication and information channels. A child who is, for example, unable to move independently or whose ability to do this is severely delayed should be given the opportunity by using aids that are available so that experiences of moving about are not denied. A child who has difficulties in perceiving sound and speech should be given information and communication not only via the ear but also at the same time through the eye and, as far as possible, through the sense of touch.

This intervention method is based on the belief that language and communication develop as an integral part of the child's overall development. This means that the acquisition of language and communication are important for learning and the use of other abilities. This often means that a child with learning disabilities becomes more language delayed than is 'necessary' because the learning disability causes, among other things, information about the environment to be processed in a less abstract way. This can also be seen when a language disordered child develops 'unnecessary' interruptions in his/her cognitive development, when the language disorder undermines the child's ability to use symbols to express important events.

The intervention method is also based on the assumption that motivation is the true drive necessary for learning to take place. Children experience joy and satisfaction when they learn to master new skills. There is no reason to believe that children with learning disabilities become less happy than children of normal intelligence. Children with learning disabilities have fewer chances to experience joy in learning new skills, since the expectations of and the demands from the environment are to a large extent adapted to normally developing children. It is therefore important from an early age to provide the child with suitably difficult activities and to have expectations on a level which can be met by the child. Expectations that are too low give as little motivation as those which are too high.

The development of language and communication is a continuous process which begins with the baby's first cry. The acquisition of language continues all through life, as long as the individual has a capacity to learn. Communication is defined here as the process whereby a person is influenced by one or more other people to produce a response of some kind. Communication can be conscious and goal-orientated, or entirely unconscious and with no objective. Communication is a social process in which a relationship between two or more individuals is a necessary prerequisite.

There are different types of communication; language is an abstract form which is well adjusted to human needs in our time and our culture. Language must be learnt, since it consists of a conventional system of symbols. There are several types of language. Spoken language is the most common form but there are also written language and sign language. Figure 1 illustrates the concept that speech is one of several tools used in language and that language is one of several forms of communication.

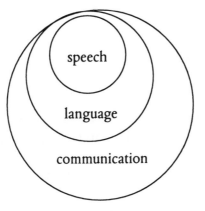

Figure 1.1. Communication, language and speech

Figure 1.1 also illustrates language acquisition, which starts from the more general and moves towards the more specific. The child develops communication before language. The early development of communication is believed to be a prerequisite of language development. There are no clear borders between different developmental stages, which means that the development is seen as a slow continuous process, where some observed advances have been prepared and learnt in part during earlier phases of development. This means that the development of communication and language processing is by necessity a prolonged process.

A child's early communication and later linguistic communication are seen as a mutually dependent unit consisting of form, content and use.

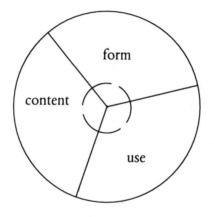

Figure 1.2. Communication and language: a unit consisting of content, form and use

The child needs some sort of tool as a means of expression in order for the development of content and use to take place. Equally, it is believed that the child's use of language and communication influences both the development of content and form. In principal, what separates the different stages of language and communication development are the different definitions given to content, form and use. The intervention method includes parallel stimulation of content, form and use.

Children with learning disability are different from children of normal intelligence. This view is of fundamental importance to the whole of this intervention method. A person with learning disability perceives and processes impressions in a manner which is not normal. The level of abstraction is lower, short term memory and perceptual ability show limits as does the ability to use knowledge already acquired in a flexible manner. The three cornerstones of this intervention method are, in short, as follows:

The stimulation should be

- **initiated early.** This means that the stimulation should start as soon after birth as possible or as soon as the parents wish. Early initiated intervention has effects which are clearly beneficial on, among other things, the establishment of early interaction patterns between parents and child.

- **carried out continuously and repetitively.** This means that the child should receive a small amount of stimulation every day and that the same activity is repeated on several consecutive days. The most important function for the therapist in this respect is to assist the parents in finding ways to make the activities an integral part of the daily routine in a natural way.

- **put together in a structured and systematic way.** This means that a defined goal behaviour is broken down into smaller components which are stimulated separately according to the normal developmental sequence. The therapist should adapt each individual activity to each individual child.

In general, the intervention method is divided into phases which correspond to different stages of language development in normal pre-school children. Only the first phase of intervention is presented in this book. The ultimate goal of the first phase is performative communication. The activities can also be seen as preparations for speech and language acquisition.

CHAPTER ONE

Training Towards Performative Communication

Performative communication can be defined as the 'speaker's' deliberate, conscious and goal-orientated use of communication (among others Snyder, 1978). The child consciously manipulates people in his/her environment in order to achieve certain goals. The communication is called imperative if the child is using a person as a tool to reach a certain goal, for example a toy which is situated out of reach. The communication is called declarative if the child uses him/herself or an object to establish social interaction with another person.

Performative communication emerges at about 10 months. Several studies show a temporal relationship between the debut of performative communication and the fifth sensory motor stage according to Piaget's developmental scale (Bates *et al.*, 1975, 1977; Harding and Golingkoff, 1979; Snyder, 1978; Greenwald and Leonard, 1979; Kahn, 1975). It is uncertain from these studies whether the sensory motor skills develop first and constitute a prerequisite for performative communication, if the relationship is the opposite or if both the performative communication and the sensory motor development reflect an underlying cognitive factor so that the relationship is only of a temporal nature. However, an experiment carried out by Steckol and Leonard (1981) supports the present intervention method's routine to stimulate sensory motor skills as a prerequisite for communicative development. Steckol and Leonard compared communicative development in three groups of children. The three groups received different intervention. The children in the first group were taught to understand how objects can be used. The children in the second group were taught to realise that objects can be used as tools in order to achieve certain goals. The children from the third group did not receive any specific training. The experiment showed that children who had been taught sensory motor skills had more developed performative communication than children who had not receive any specific training.

Performative communication is initiated when the child is able to vary his/her communicative expressions deliberately to reach specific goals. The form that performative communication takes is a coordination of body movements, arm and hand movements, gaze or eye contact and sound. The gradual development of the performative expressions are seen in increasing complexity, specialisation and symbol content (Lindström and Thurfjell, 1985). The development of the early forms of communicative expressions is a gradual process which is connected with the child's neuromotor and cognitive development. The neuromotor development determines which movements the child is able to carry out. Crudely, the development starts with the child's early occasional movements which are characterised by poor control, precision and coordination and moves towards the successive coordination of movements with an increasing degree of complexity, precision and differentiation of the coordinators. Cognitive development determines how the child arranges his/her movements according to, for example, conventional patterns. To be able to express intention and goal orientation, the form of expression needs to be arranged in a way which is easily recognised and understood. The child must arrange his/her expressions within the framework of a larger communication act, where certain events precede certain other events. The child also needs to be able to anticipate the response from the other person.

The activities presented in this book are in one way or another preparations for the overall goal – performative communication. The arrangement of activities is explained broadly below.

THE INTERACTION

Preparatory speech and language intervention should start during the baby's first month of life. The strongest motivation for this is the belief that an early established positive interaction between the child and the adult is the foundation upon which further communication and linguistic development is built. This belief is supported by certain psychological theories which emphasize a harmonious relationship between the child and the adult in the total development of the child. In order for a harmonious relationship to become established between the child and the adult one condition is that there should exist a mutual 'understanding'; this, among other things, demands communication. It is a paradox that the harmonious relationship is also seen as a condition for the development of communication.

In normal circumstances it is assumed that the mother has a biological readiness to interact with her baby in a normal manner. If the newborn baby for some reason does not fulfil the mother's expectations, for example if the baby's expressions are fainter and to some extent different or the expressions develop at abnormal times, which is the case in Down's Syndrome (Buckhalt *et al.*, 1978; Cicchetti and Sroufe, 1976, 1978; Dunst, 1981; Cythryn, 1975; Emde *et al.*, 1978), it is assumed that the maternal readiness gets out of step with the baby's signals and expressions. The mutual 'understanding' fails to occur or is made more difficult to establish. This also applies to the first steps towards the early establishment of an harmonious relationship.

This intervention method is focused to a large extent on developing early interaction patterns between the adult and the baby. Against this background we suggest using alternative communication channels such as the tactile and visual channels by using gestures to augment and to complement the audio-vocal channel, as well as training the adult's sensitivity to the baby's signals and their understanding of their own conscious over-interpretation of these signals.

The possible delay between the adult's readiness and the baby's expressions may be compensated for by the early establishment of tactile communication. Therefore the adult is encouraged to give the baby body massage many times a day, preferably using massage oil. Experience shows that the baby responds in an obvious way, using body movements, while the adult carries out the massage. The massage, which becomes a daily routine during the first year, provides contact between the child and the adult as well as important 'by-products', for example the baby's tactile sensitivity is stimulated which slowly leads to increasing body awareness.

It is useful to regard communication development as a social process. The development is determined and influenced by the prevailing overall culture and its subcultures. This means that a child in our country is influenced by the western culture but also by the private culture which exists within the family. This is obvious when different cultures' communication patterns are compared. The tactile communication channel is scarcely used in our culture compared with many so-called primitive cultures. Sörenson (1979) described the interaction between children and adults in a region of New Guinea, where the people were relatively isolated from the surrounding world. The children in this culture receive almost constant body contact with another person for as long as they wish. Tactile communication is developed between the child and the adult long before the children start to talk. These children receive different sensory stimulation from children in the western world. This leads to another type of emotional, perceptual and cognitive structuring in these children which is shown by, for example, the rarity or absence of frustration reactions, according to Sörenson.

In an harmonious relationship both the child and the grown-up feel a sense of security in the mutual understanding and approachability which is present in the relationship. This sense of security may encourage the child to explore the surrounding world which leads to gained knowledge and experiences about relationships and objects in the environment. This is important for further communicative and linguistic development. In addition, the sense of security provides both the child and the adult with a favourable communication climate since one major factor for the development of dialogue is the ability to adjust.

The timing and duration of a baby's activities tend to mirror those of its mother. In a newborn baby, this appears as simultaneity in the rhythmic activity of the adult and the baby (Condon & Sanders, 1974; Condon, 1979; Brazelton et al., 1974). For example, a long utterance from the mother may be mirrored by prolonged movements by the baby. The child's ability to adjust to other people is thought to emerge at this stage. The simultaneous activities present in the newborn baby develop into reciprocal turn-taking when the baby is about four months old; this forms the basis for the development of complex and abstract linguistic dialogue (Bullowa et al., 1976; Stern et al., 1975; Schaffer et al., 1977).

The baby shows other signs of adjustment to communication and interaction with people as early as the first few months of life. At about two months of age a baby following normal developmental patterns behaves differently, depending on whether he/she is on his/her own, is with other people, or is playing with objects (Trevarthen, 1979; Brazelton et al., 1974). A crude grouping of the environment into the groups human and non-human seems to direct the baby's actions. The child communicates with the group human and acts on the group non-human. The baby's sound production as well as the frequency with which the child looks at the mother's face is increased when the mother is generally more active (and especially when she is talking to the child) compared with situations when she is more passive (Rheingold *et al.*, 1959; Stern, 1974; Stern *et al.*, 1975). It is against this background that we encourage the adult to talk frequently to their baby in addition to helping the baby to manipulate and explore objects. The development of communication, like other areas of development, demands a lot of practice for the skills to develop. A child with learning disability is believed to be less able to take initiatives and therefore the adult needs to help the child to initiate different activities.

This intervention method encourages frequent conversations between the adult and the baby for another reason as well. The adult as well as the child needs training and experiences of interaction to be able to notice and correctly identify the child's signals and to be able to adjust his/her communication to a suitable level for the child. In order for the adult to have adequate expectations of and make suitable demands on their child, it is important that the therapist informs the adult about normal development and puts the adult's fears into context with realistic expectations of the child's development. It is also important to identify the child's signals in conjunction with the adult. Some signals, such as eye contact and smiles, appear to be more important than others. Eye contact and gaze provide information about, for example, attention and interest. The smile provides information about the emotional aspects of interaction. The smile is a positive signal which the adult interprets to mean that the baby is experiencing satisfaction. The smile is therefore of great importance for the early stages of communicative interaction, since it is also a signal for continued interaction. Parents of Down's Syndrome children should be told that the social smile appears later and less frequently with a less marked facial expression in children with Down's Syndrome (Chicchetti & Sroufe, 1976, 1978; Dunst, 1981; Buckhalt *et al.*, 1978; Emde *et al.*, 1978; Cythyn, 1975) than in children with normal development.

Maternal responsiveness, maternal attentiveness, maternal interaction and physical contact are factors which are often seen as important parameters for the normal development of communication (Cohen & Beckwith, 1979; Freedle & Lewis, 1977). In normal circumstances these factors are thought to be adopted automatically and the baby receives sufficient amounts of these factors for normal development to take place. This adaptation of the adult to the baby also includes the adult's way of talking to the baby. This is known as Baby Talk. The adult (or other people older than the child) talks to the baby in a manner different from that when the adult is talking to another adult or an older child. This is shown in all the different dimensions of speech and language – semantics, syntax, lexicon, morphology, phonology, prosody and pure pronunciation factors (among others Newport *et al.*, 1977; Cross, 1977). This process is an unconscious and very natural part of communication with children and it is probably controlled by the adult's apprehension of the child, based on the responses (or rather the adult's ability to interpret the responses) which the baby gives when communicating.

In an harmonious relationship, the adult and the child both show an interest in each other's activities. This can be seen as the cornerstone for the development of mutual reference. The adult and the child who take part in each other's activities build up mutual experiences. The adult often intuitively knows what the child might express and in addition what the child cannot 'talk' about. The mutual experience makes it possible for the adult to know the limits of the child's knowledge and experiences of the environment. It is with this knowledge about the child that the adult is able to make interpretations of content and function of the child's communicative expressions in a manner which is beneficial for the child's development.

We encourage the adult to make conscious interpretations and over-interpretations of the child's signals and expressions. By doing this the adult is aware of the child's attention and actions long before the stage in the child's development when the child engages the adult in his/her activities. The child's actions become shared and mutual activities through the adult's involvement. In this way the child is not only being prepared for mutual attention but also prepared for deliberate communication, since the adult makes interpretations of purpose and goal in the child's expressions which do not have a goal. The adult recognises some of the child's expressions and interprets them as if they were directed to the adult, then the adult responds to the expressions in a manner appropriate for the interpretation. For example, the baby is crying in a certain way and the adult responds by changing the baby's nappy, feeding or hugging the baby. It is assumed that the child develops chains of associations between his/her own expressions and the responses they provoke in the adult and that this may be important for the development of expectation and the order of sequences of actions and activities.

Communication is an interaction in which development also depends on the responses which are provided. Bullowa *et al.* (1976) highlight the importance of an encouraging and positive attitude from the environment towards the child's communicative and linguistic development. This attitude is believed to be particularly important if the child has auditory difficulties or motor delay which lead to difficulties in processing communicative expressions in a normal manner. Many children with Down's Syndrome have auditory processing difficulties. It is therefore important to provide these children with answers which are very explicit. We emphasise the importance of using gestures, facial expressions and signs as an early complement to speech.

It is also vital that the child is given ample opportunity for positive interaction because it is during such contact that the child's image of him/herself – that is, his/her identity – is shaped and reshaped (Mead (1934) 1967). The child perceives his/her self through reactions from other persons. A favourably disposed environment gives the child a positive self-image to a greater extent than an unfavourably disposed environment. Communication plays an important role in several ways, for example, it involves ongoing role-reversal situations.

Through this role-reversal it is thought that the child sees him/herself through the other person's eyes more easily and incorporates the other person's impressions. The role-reversal may also make it easier for the child to understand that other people do not have the same experiences as the child. The child starts to take the other person's perspective. Without this development of understanding it would be difficult for the child to develop towards performative communication with goal-orientated, conscious manipulations of other people and situations.

VISION

The psychological importance of eye contact for communication cannot be over-valued and it is generally known that actively gaining eye contact with a baby also provides interactive contact. A child with learning disability should be given structured stimulation of vision and eye contact as early as possible, not only for the development of communication but also for the child's general development. The visual stimulation should be intensive during the baby's first months and the stimulation should include different visual functions.

It is important for the adult to make a habit of seeking, gaining and keeping eye contact with the baby for as long as possible to initiate a communication act. The eye contact signals have an initiating function for communication but are also important for keeping the conversation going and ending the conversation. Eye contact is perhaps the most important tool in early communication for controlling the other person's attention, interest, receptiveness and communicative motivation. The adult is generally very sensitive to variations in the child's eye contact.

The suggested visual stimulation is structured to encourage togetherness and mutual participation during activities. This is based on descriptions of the normal visual development where mutual gaze is believed to be fundamental for future visual development. The gaze, as a tool for attention, and attention itself, are thought to have a mutual or shared function. The function is mutual when the adult and the child look at each other. The function is shared when the adult and the child look at the same object or activity. The gaze is then attributed to a third function – the deictic – when the gaze is used as a tool to draw the other person's attention towards an event or an object.

Shared gaze and attention appear only after mutual gaze and attention have been established. For this the baby needs to be able to transfer his/her attention from a person to an object. At about four months in normal development the baby is highly person-orientated in his/her attention during communication. The baby looks at the adult's face during the majority of the interaction. After some time the baby seems more interested in objects and activities. The baby's attention has become object-orientated and this is shown by the fact that the baby looks at the adult only for a small fraction of the interaction time. At this stage the baby does not pay attention to the adult but the adult follows the baby's actions and acts as if he/she was part of the baby's centre of attention by naming what the baby is looking at. By doing this the adult is getting ready for the next stage when the child starts an interaction about an activity or with the adult by switching eye contact from the adult to the activity or the object.

Mutual eye contact and mutual attention are important for the development of turn-taking skills in conversations when the baby and the adult take it in turns to express themselves and listen to each other. Mutual gaze and mutual attention are similarly important for the development of a joint reference and it is therefore an important step in the development towards performative communication.

Gaze is also an important tool for the child to use to gain knowledge and experiences which lie outside the development of communication. This aspect also motivates early visual stimulation for children with learning disability since the ability to use selective attention is vital for the learning process. This means that the child has to learn to focus both his/her eye gaze and attention on the activities and the objects which are important at that moment in time and to ignore all other activities.

LISTENING

It is common that children with learning disabilities perceive, process and interpret auditory information in an abnormal way. Many children with, for example, Down's Syndrome, have complex auditory difficulties and various studies suggest that these children perceive and interpret visual information more easily than auditory information (e.g. Bateman & Wetherell, 1965). The goal of our method is for the children to develop speech. It is therefore important to provide the child with intensive and conscious stimulation of the auditory function in addition to alternative ways of communicating.

The adult is encouraged to converse in a structured way with the baby on a daily basis. These conversations should be carried out in a manner which also incorporates other interactive functions, such as turn-taking. The purpose is not only to facilitate the development of fundamental discrimination between sounds which are important for speech but also to train the child to recognise sound patterns. This is believed to help the child to be able to focus his/her auditory attention. It is a way of training selective listening to sound patterns important for speech.

The auditory stimulation is based on studies of normal development (e.g. Kuhl, 1979; Eilers *et al.*, 1977) and studies of children with Down's Syndrome (Johansson, 1983a, b). During normal development the baby responds very early to sound differences which are later important for speech recognition. It has been shown that some sound differences are easier for the baby to recognise than others. There is a certain order in which the child learns to discriminate between sounds. Here are a few examples. At one to four months of age the baby reacts to difference between /pa/ – /ba/; at six to eight months the baby reacts to the difference between /sa/ – /za/ and not until the age of 12 to 14 months does the child react to the difference between /fi/ – /θi/. Children with Down's Syndrome show a significant delay in the ability to discriminate auditory information. This is already obvious during the first six months.

It is a common experience that speech and language disordered children have a history of less advanced babbling which occurs less frequently. This is the case for, for example, children with Down's Syndrome, even if some aspects of their babbling seem to follow normal developmental patterns (Johansson 1983c, 1985). The latter part of the auditory stimulation programme has a somewhat different goal from the early stages. The activities are structured and are based on some aspects of the normal development of babbling (among others Oller, 1978; Stark 1980). The baby produces more sounds when the adult is talking to him/her and very early on adapts his/her sound production to match the adult's sounds (Rheingold *et al.*, 1958; Delack, 1975). The adult's sound production is believed to amplify the baby's own sound production as a part of the baby's ability to 'mirror' and later on to imitate the adult.

MOTOR SKILLS

Every type of communication act is a signal. A signal is produced by a movement even if this movement is very small. Motor skills are therefore a necessity for communication. One of the fundamental ideas behind our intervention method states that communicative and linguistic development take place under the influence of the child's general development and, among other areas, this also applies to motor development.

Different gross motor skills are thought to be important for the development of communication in both a direct and an indirect way. Indirectly, the motor development influences communication development since the child gains knowledge about the environment through his/her body and activities (Piaget, e.g. 1952). Both the child's own movements and the child's perception of movements in other people, animals and objects are important, firstly for the child's growing knowledge about objects and the relationship between them, and secondly for the development of the ability to experience order in a sequence of events. By his/her actions the child is believed to gain knowledge to enable him/her to recognise some aspects in the environment which are predictable. The child starts to recognise properties of the environment when some events are repeated in a similar way. The child starts to experience regularity as certain activities are repeated in a similar way. The child discovers, for example, that one object can be present under different circumstances and that there are several objects of the same kind, although they are not identical. This is a beginning of the child's understanding of object constancy, object functions and of other properties of objects. These discoveries are believed to occur when the baby observes objects in motion which has been initiated by the child him/herself or by someone or something else. Probably all the observations which the child makes when he/she moves about are equally important. A more direct influence by the gross motor skills on communication development occurs when a certain disorder hinders other skills which are important for the development of communication. If, for example, the child is unable to keep his/her body upright, some coordinated expressions between eye and hand are hindered. This assumption is based on experiments carried out by Bower (1974). The experiments showed that normally developing babies at 7 to 14 days already looked at and oriented their bodies towards an object positioned in the body's midline, provided the babies were held in an upright position. This coordination between vision and body movement does not normally appear before the age of about four months or whenever the baby starts to sit up. Thus one function, the upright position, previously thought to be of little significance for communication development, seems to have a coordinating function of great importance.

In our intervention method, gross motor activities are not mentioned. It is assumed that the child is receiving physiotherapy on a regular basis. One example of how the gross motor training can be structured for a girl with Down's syndrome during her first year of life is described by Åkerström (1986).

During the continued communication and language stimulation which follows after the initial intervention phase – towards performative communication – the child's hand function becomes the most powerful tool for language. Hand stimulation is needed for the hands to function satisfactorily as a language tool. The goal during the first year is for general good hand motor function in addition to the beginning of a growing knowledge of what the hands can be used for.

Hand function is also important for the development of performative communication. For example, it can have an indirect as well as a direct effect. Performative communication is based on self-awareness and the child's abilities in relation to other people. The child needs to experience him/herself in comparison with the surrounding world. Therefore, the child needs to develop self-awareness as a constant factor and the child's own body movements partly develop this awareness. The child's active interaction is believed to assist this process and is seen in the child's ability to reach for an object (reaching up, down, forward, towards the side, using one arm, etc.), grasping the object, handling it in different ways and letting go of the object (Kinney, 1979). The hand and the arm become the important tool with which the child measures distances and directions to objects using his/her own body as a reference point.

It is probably highly important that the adult starts to point out objects and events to the child early on and also physically assists the child to point. Pointing serves several important functions in the child's development. Pointing is, among other things, one of the more advanced forms of expression in performative communication. Pointing is important as a deictic signal and is used for shared attention. Pointing is used earlier on for functions other than the deictic during normal development. The child points for him/herself as an aid to identifying entities in the real world and clarifying them. The pointing is at this stage seen as a tool which the child uses to single out him/herself from the surroundings and at the same time to develop the ability to make reference.

The ability to point shows a successive development, as do other early communicative expressions. Escalona (1974) describes pointing during normal development as being initiated at three to four months when the adult points to an object in front of the child and describes the object. At approximately six to seven months the baby takes an object on his/her own initiative; the adult interprets this act by assuming that the child wants the adult to describe the object. The adult acts according to his/her interpretation of the child's motive whereby a chain reaction occurs. When the child grasps an object, the adult provides a description. When the child is seven to eight months old the adult starts to point in order to direct the child's attention. It is interesting to note that the child only manages to follow a pointing movement several months later with his/her eyes if it crosses the child's midline (Murphy & Messer, 1977). Not until approximately 12 months does the child start to use pointing in order to direct the adult's attention.

The child's handling of objects is important in order for the child to gain knowledge about the world. The child learns how different objects feel according to their weight, form, size and surface texture. The child also learns what he/she can do with objects. This is a developmental sequence which, in principle, has its counterpart in other areas of development, for example in the development of sounds. There are temporal agreements which make it plausible that development in different behaviour areas is determined by a joint set of cognitive factors. This may possibly mean that learning in one area leads to some sort of transfer effect into other areas. The child's handling of objects (Sinclair, 1970) develops from non-specific short activities towards serially ordered sequences where several objects are exposed to the same handling and even later towards a diversity by object-specific handling in every sequence of events. The child initially grasps and handles all objects in the same manner one at a time. At a later stage the child throws three different objects which happen to lie on the table down on the floor. At an even later stage the child stacks bricks but rolls a ball. The cognitive development which directs this change makes it possible for the child to link several isolated activities into one large activity and at a later stage vary smaller parts within a larger activity. The child's handling of objects is not only easy to observe but also easy to take part in. The adult is therefore encouraged to stimulate the child's exploration of objects in various ways.

PLAY

The definition of performative communication as an intentional, conscious and goal-oriented activity means the use of certain expressions as tools to reach certain goals. The child needs to be flexible, since known goals may need new tools and old tools may be used to reach new goals. Important prerequisites are a certain awareness of object-constancy and how objects are related in reality, for example the cause and effect relationship.

One of the fundamental principles behind our intervention method is that all stimulation should take place in a play activity if at all possible even if the play activity itself is structured. During play, interaction skills and important pragmatic skills are stimulated. For example, during play the child learns to listen and follow instructions and reply according to the instruction given.

The child learns important aspects of object-constancy in peekaboo and hiding games. Hiding games have different features at different ages during normal development (Bower, 1974). At six months the child is able to find a completely hidden object only if he/she has seen the object being hidden and there is only one hiding place. At 12 months the child finds the hidden object even if there are several hiding places but only if he/she has again seen the object being hidden. It is not until 18 months that the child finds a hidden object without having seen the object being hidden. The child is now believed to have an inner representation of the object and to have reached a certain understanding of the object's own existence.

Of importance for the development of the understanding of cause and effect and other aspects of the relationship of objects is the knowledge the child develops during simple games like 'put the objects in a box' or 'pull the table cloth to reach the cake'. For example, it is probably important for the child to experience the same pattern of actions being used with different objects or one object being handled in different ways. By repeating actions – during play and when interacting with another person – the child gains knowledge about what objects are used for. During interaction with the adult the child learns about his/her own and other persons' limitations and abilities. In the simplest form of 'give and take' the child is stimulated by different roles in communication by being the provider (of objects or messages) or the receiver (of objects or messages).

These games are structured in a manner which makes the child not only able to experience him/herself and others as the cause of an action but also the one who receives the action or the effects of the action. The games are structured in a manner which makes the objects disappear and reappear in different ways. The child's actions during these games or the child's knowledge about actions in these games is reflected not only in the child's performative communication but also later during the child's language development. The fundamental structure in the hiding game is also found later on in the early language development of linear phrases, where an object word is combined with a relation type word with the functions *existence* (there, look), *disappearance* (gone, finished) or *recurrence* (more, again) (Bloom & Lahey, 1978). The fundamental relationship during the child's play between the person who starts an activity and the effects of this activity reoccur somewhat later in the early language development where *agent, patient* and *recipient* appear as primary semantic groupings (Bloom & Lahey, 1978).

IMITATION

Imitation is often perceived as a very important aspect of the child's learning of different functions, among others the communicative and linguistic functions (for example Bates *et al.*, 1979). The imitation is seen above all as the tool which the child uses in new unknown behaviours. Many children with learning disability, among others children with Down's Syndrome (Ekström & Johansson, 1986) find imitation difficult. This is not surprising, since imitation is a complex process. The child must have the ability to perceive an expression and remember it during shorter or longer periods of time, in order finally to recreate the same pattern in his/her own production.

In our intervention method much emphasis is placed on pure imitation stimulation. This stimulation is focused, above all, on imitation of movements during the stages which are presented in this book and they should be carried out simultaneously with physical help from an adult. Another reason for this approach is that the child is believed to recognise movement patterns which he/she has experienced in his/her own activities. This idea is similar to the notion that communication and language development take place within the framework of the relationship between the understanding of what other people do and say and the child's own production and use of communication and language.

The imitation stimulation is structured on the basis of knowledge about normal development. The earliest communication is characterized by simultaneity in the baby's and the adult's activities. The simultaneous act also contains similarities between the baby's and the adult's type of expression. This is popularly described as the baby 'mirroring' the adult, for example in fundamental frequency, tongue, jaw and lip movements (Meltzoff & Moore, 1977; Trevarthen, 1979). These 'mirroring' activities only contain movements which the baby has already carried out on his/her own and it is not believed that the baby learns new behaviours through these early imitations.

The simultaneity and the similarity in expressions are viewed here as the foundation from which imitation develops. As a result, therefore, we stress the importance of mutuality, sharing and simultaneity (or alternative patterns) during the interaction between the baby and the adult.

CHAPTER TWO

The Project 'Early Language Intervention in Children with Down's Syndrome'

This chapter presents the development of Down's Syndrome children in Sweden who underwent early language intervention. A small group of these children were observed on a monthly basis using a specially designed assessment form. The assessments covered the development of communication, cognitive, social and motor skills. There was only one criterion for the selection of children, which was the date when they started taking part in the project. The observed children differed in their medical histories, cognitive skills and social backgrounds. The group consisted of children both with and without additional handicaps. For example, several children went through heart surgery during the project period. The children lived at home with their parents, apart from two who had been placed in foster homes. The children received the early language intervention from the parents (or foster parents) during the period when the parents were on maternity/paternity leave (i.e., during the child's first 18 months). After this period most of the children started to attend day care facilities, for example a creche or a childminder, or they stayed at home if their parents worked at home. At this stage most of the children received language intervention from a person other than their own parents, although the intervention was carried out in consultation with the parents and was followed-up in the home environment. The situations, and hence the intervention, varied for each child. Some children were lucky, as they had a personal assistant at their creche who took responsibility for carrying out the stimulation, while other staff members followed up the stimulation whenever appropriate in daily activities. Other children were not so lucky, since the staff at their creche followed the policy that all children should be treated in the same way, regardless of any specific additional needs. In these circumstances the signing did not work out well. For most children who were looked after by a childminder the situations were favourable.

The observations only show when skills started to appear. It is important to mention that the observations do not provide information about qualitative or quantitative aspects of development. The observations should also be viewed in general rather than specific terms, since they were collected by the parents in collaboration with the children's Speech and Language Therapist. The observations were carried out once a month.

Some observations have not been recorded fully (tables 3,4,5 and 6). The most common reason for the missing data was illness or forgetfulness, although another cause was uncertainty as to when observed skills emerged. The median values have been presented for the group as a whole in addition to the earliest and latest appearance of skills.

The goal for phase one of early language intervention was *performative communication*. This goal was reached by the project children with only one month's delay compared to children developing normally. Other important features of early communication skills were also reached after a similar delay by the project children compared to normal developmental patterns. In Table 1 the median values of the project children's early communication development are compared to normal developmental averages. The comparative data was collected from studies by Capute *et al.* (1981) and Bates *et al.* (1977). Capute *et al.* studied the language development of a large number of normally developing children in order to find a developmental norm to use for clinical diagnosis of children at risk.

Of the four 'cornerstones' in early communication development which are compared in Table 1, the project children showed no delay in the appearance of reduplicated babbling, and a small delay in the ability to turn towards a voice and in the use of performative communication. A larger delay was seen in the appearance of isolated spoken words (four to six words). The project children's use of isolated spoken words took place three months later than in normal development. However, it should be stressed that the project children developed symbol capacity mostly through signing.

Table 1. Comparison of early communicative development
in project children and normally developing children.
Ages given in months.

	Project children	Normal development	
		Capute et al. 1981	Bates et al. 1977
Orienting towards voice	5	4	
Reduplicated babbling*	8	8	
Performative communication*	11		10
Single words	18	15	

* For a more detailed comparison and description see Johansson (1983,1985) and Lindstroem and Thurfjell (1985).

It is hard to find comparative data on the spontaneous development of early communication skills in Down's Syndrome children. It is therefore difficult to discuss the effects of intervention during these early developmental stages. There are, however, clear indications that the Down's Syndrome children on the project gained from early intervention. These are shown in Table 1 and also in the comparison of the test results of a language assessment (SILD, Ekstroem & Johansson, 1986) carried out on the project children and a control group of Down's Syndrome children. The comparative assessment showed that the children who did not receive early intervention managed only 50–60 % of all the test activities which the project children of the same age managed fully.

In Table 2 some aspects of the early development of the project children are shown.

Table 2. The early development of project children

Age in months	Communication	Cognitive/Social	Fine motor	Gross motor
6–7	Shows satisfaction in social interaction	Shows recognition of parents	Reaches and grasps an object	Rolls
	Gains attention by making sounds	Looks for a long time at own image in a mirror	Takes an object which is in front of him/her	Reaches one arm forward while lying on stomach
			Holds two objects, one in each hand	Sits with support
8–9	Reduplicated babbling	Removes towel from face	Transfers object from one hand to the other	Moves around his/her axis
	Reacts appropriately to signal gestures	Looks for objects which disappears	Picks up small objects	Sits without support
			Thumb-finger grip	
10–11	Performative communication	Actively takes part in peekaboo		Crawls
	Reacts adequately to signal word	Imitates		
	Imitates sounds and movement	Shakes sound toy to make sound		
12–13		Finds an object which was hidden while the child watched	Uses index finger to explore	Rotates body

		Picks up objects from a box	Claps hands	Changes position from sitting to lying and crawling to sitting
14–15	Protowords	Puts objects in box Opens box to find object Rolls and catches ball	Uses crayons	Side-steps with support Walks when supported in both hands
16–17	Points to nose, eye, mouth when requested		Pincer grip	Crawls up a slope
18–19	Isolated single words			Walks with support to one hand

To some extent the data in Table 2 correspond to descriptions of normal early development (for example Alin-Åkerman, 1982; Alin-Åkerman & Nordberg, 1980).

It is seen as normal that

- the six to seven month old child studies his/her own image in a mirror with interest, discriminates between parents and strangers, looks at falling objects, takes objects which are held out, transfers objects from one hand to the other and moves around his/her axis.

- the eight to nine month old child shakes a rattle to produce a sound, imitates, for example, waving, sits without support and stands with support.

- the 10 to 11 month old child picks up a toy from a box, finds objects which are hidden while he/she watches, claps hands, points using his/her index finger, crawls, takes sidesteps and walks with support.

- the 12 to 13 month old child rolls a ball, puts objects in a box and walks a few steps without support.

The project children showed a greater delay in motor development than in communication and cognitive development compared with normal development. The delay was obvious in the appearance of the pincer grip which normally appears at 10 months compared with 16–17 months for the project children and the ability to walk without support which normally takes place at 12–13 months but occured at 21 months in the project children. In one respect the project children actually developed one skill earlier than normal. This was the ability to point to three body parts when requested, for example eye, nose and mouth. The project children did this at 16–17 months. According to the Griffith test (Alin-Åkerman & Nordberg, 1980) this is a suitable test task for 22 months.

Table 3. Project children's communicative development
(Ages given in months)

	median	lowest age	highest age	number
Orients towards voice	5	3	8	17
Shows satisfaction in social interaction	6	5	9	19
Gains attention by making sound variations (not crying)	7	5	12	20
Reacts appropriately to signal gestures (come, up, look)	8	6	13	20
Reduplicated babbling	8	6	11	20
Reacts appropriately to signal words (hello, come, look)	10	8	17	21
Performative communication	11	8	18	20
Imitates sound	11	7	18	15
Protowords	14	9	20	16
Points when requested to three body parts (eye, nose, mouth)	17	13	25	15
Isolated spoken words	18	13	25	17

Table 4. Project children's cognitive and social development
(Ages given in months)

	median	lowest age	highest age	number
Shows recognition of parents	6	5	9	17
Studies own image in mirror	6	5	12	20
Removes towel from eyes (during play)	8	5	13	21
Looks for an object which disappears out of view	8	5	13	20
Active participation in peekaboo	10	8	17	21
Imitates movements	11	8	17	22
Shakes rattle to make a sound	11	8	17	20
Picks up object from a box	12	9	17	22
Finds object which was hidden while he/ she was watching (one hiding place)	12	8	17	21
Puts objects in a box	14	10	17	23
Opens box to find toy	14	11	17	21
Rolls/catches ball	14	10	15	19
Holds up arms and legs when getting dressed and undressed	15	12	20	16

Table 5. Project children's hand motor development
(Ages given in months)

	median	lowest age	highest age	number
Takes an object which is held in front of him/her	6	5	9	14
Reaches for and grasps an object	6	5	10	18
Holds two objects, one in each hand	7	5	11	18
Moves object from one hand to the other	8	5	11	17
Lets go of one object in order to pick up another	8	5	11	19
Picks up small objects from table using palmar grasp	8	6	10	17
Picks up small objects using thumb-finger grasp	9	6	14	19
Uses index finger to explore objects	13	8	22	22
Claps hands	13	9	18	22
Makes marks on paper with crayon	14	10	27	19
Pincer grip	16	8	27	20

Table 6. Project children's gross motor development
(Ages given in months)

	median	lowest age	highest age	number
Supports body on arms, lifts head and chest when lying on stomach	6	3	10	17
Reaches one arm forward when lying on stomach	6	5	10	16
Able to keep body in crawling position for a short while	9	7	16	17
Protects him/herself when falling forward	10	8	20	16
Protects him/herself when falling sideways	10	8	17	17
Rocks backwards and forwards in crawling position	10	8	16	15
Reaches one hand forward while in crawling position	11	8	17	11
Reaches one hand forward while standing	11	7	20	15
Rotates body while standing	13	9	17	13
Rolls from side to back	5	3	9	17
Rolls from side to side	6	5	9	17
Rolls from back to side	6	5	9	17
Rolls from stomach to back	6	5	12	18
Rolls from back to stomach	8	5	14	17
Moves around his/her own axis while sitting on floor	8	5	13	18
Crawls	10	8	14	16
Crawls with stomach lifted from floor	14	10	20	12
Takes side steps while supporting hands on furniture	14	9	18	13
Walks when supported in both hands	14	10	21	14
Crawls up stairs	17	11	27	11
Walks when supported by one hand	18	12	27	12
Sits with support	7	5	9	17
Sits while supported by own arms	8	5	15	19
Sits in high chair	9	6	15	16
Sits without support	9	7	15	16
Changes from lying to sitting position	12	7	15	16
Changes from sitting to standing position	13	8	17	16
Changes from sitting to crawling position	12	9	21	14
Sits down with support	13	9	17	13

PART TWO

Practical Advice and Activities

Introduction

The suggested activities which are presented in this book are divided into 12 'programmes'. The programmes are numbered in the sequence they have been presented to the project children. Each programme contains activities to cover approximately one month of stimulation with weekly changes of activity.

It is important to stress that the activities presented have suited many of the 58 project children. However, none of the children have followed all activities in detail.

Fundamental rules for stimulation:

1. All children are different and live in different environments. Therefore activities need to be adapted to each individual child.

2. The adult who takes responsibility for the stimulation has to be aware that both patience and determination are required. The therapist's role is to encourage and support the adult and above all help the adult to notice the child's achievements.

3. The stimulation should take place on a daily basis.

4. Every activity should be repeated daily for about a week. The stimulation should take place in as quiet and non-distracting environment as possible.

5. Every activity should be carried out in its entirety. This means that the adult helps the child to complete the activity to a large extent.

6. The activities should be carried out in a manner which the child finds enjoyable. The child should have fun.

7. The child should never be forced to carry out an activity when he/she lacks the motivation. The adult needs to be sensitive to the child's reactions. In addition, the adult needs to be able to arouse the child's interest and motivation for the activities.

8. The child should often be praised in a manner which the child understands. The child is **never** given negative feedback in connection with the activities.

WEEK 1

1   Children learn to perceive differences between sounds from a very early age. This is fundamental to the development of speech perception at a later stage. Some children, for example most children with Down's Syndrome, are less able to respond to variations in sounds. These children should be stimulated on a daily basis to listen to differences in sounds and to focus their attention towards various sound sources.

Therefore, at first the child should be stimulated to perceive the fundamental rhythms of spoken English. Talk to your child in a special way for short intervals every day. Try to make this a routine so that you talk in this way in certain situations, for example each time you change nappies.

Repeat the syllable 'da' very many times this week. Pronounce the syllable clearly and slowly, making the 'a' very long. Try to pronounce the syllable slowly every time.

From now on a long, clearly pronounced syllable will be shown like this:

' dā '

If you want to vary the sound you can also use long and clear 'ba' or 'gu' syllables. Remember to make the syllables long.

This activity may seem tedious to you, but it is a different experience for the child. He/she may need many repetitions to be able to recognise the rhythms which are used every week.

2   Make it a routine to give your child body massage during the first year. Rub the child all over every day according to a set pattern. Either use a towel or even better use your fingers. This is one order in which you could massage your child:

head, nose, cheeks, mouth, forehead, ears, chin, chest, arms, hands, stomach, hips, legs, feet, back of the head, back, buttocks, legs, soles of the feet.

If you turn the massage into a daily routine you will make it easier for your child to get to know his/her own body. This is fundamental for body awareness, which in itself is important for understanding the surrounding world.

You should also get used to talking to your child often. Sometimes it can be hard to find something to talk about. Since a great deal of our behaviour is based on routine, it is suggested that while massaging your child you pronounce the sound rhythms. When doing this you are strengthening your child's experience of rhythm.

3   Make use of all opportunities to catch and keep eye contact with your child. When eye contact is steady, start to guide the gaze of your child with your own gaze. Try the following:

- The child is lying on its back on your lap.

- Establish eye contact. Talk, sing, babble or repeat the rhythm (activity 1) and at the same time move your head to one side. Do not break the eye contact.

- If your child is not following your eyes, hold the child's chin and carefully turn his/her head slightly in the same direction.

- Repeat the movement towards the other side.

4   Mirrors are excellent for all children. Consider getting a large mirror to put on the wall next to the child's bed or changing table or any other place where he/she often spends time. A mirror reflects light and movement in an interesting way.

WEEK 2

1   Continue to talk to your child in rhythms. This week the syllable ('de','da', 'bu', or 'ba') is very short. From now on a short syllable will be shown like this:

' dǎ '

2   The body massage continues on a daily basis for a long, long time to come. Massage rhythmically at the same time as you say the sounds described in activity 1. One effect of the massage is stimulation of the sense of touch. Let your child experience many opportunities to stimulate this sense. Put the undressed child on various contrasting surfaces; soft-rough surfaces, warm–cool surfaces and so on.

3   Continue to catch and keep eye contact with your child as often and for as long as you can. Vary the visual stimulation, for example by using a number of materials in and around the child's bed. Use a variety of single-coloured and multi-coloured fabrics. Yellow, red and orange are colours which small children usually like.

WEEK 3

1   By now you have probably found situations which are suitable for the stimulation of rhythms for your baby. Carry on being very careful to look straight into the eyes of the child when you are pronouncing the rhythms. Lean over your child so that your face is close to his/her face (about eight inches may be a suitable distance). As soon as the eyes of the child meet yours persist in trying to 'stick fast' to the child's eyes and keep the eye contact for as long as possible. This is important, because it will tell you when your child is listening to you.

Let the child listen repeatedly every day to the following rhythm variation:

dādādā dădădă dādādā

Start off by saying the very long and clear syllable. Repeat this syllable in the same manner until you are certain the child is listening to you. When this happens change to saying the very short syllable many times over until you are certain the child is listening. Then change back to the long syllable again. Continue like this for as long as you can keep his/her attention. This means that you can gradually extend the time the child is capable of listening to you.

2   Body massage and stimulation of the sense of touch continues in the same way as last week.

3   Encourage the child to follow a luminous point or an object with the eyes.

Material: a torch with a thin piece of paper over the front to soften the beam.

Try the following:

- The child is lying on its back on your lap.

- When you have established eye contact move the softened light beam into the child's field of view.

- The child is now looking at the torch light. Move the light beam to one side, like you did earlier with your head.

- Continue the activity as you did last week. Brightly coloured toys can be used in the same way as the torch.

4 Some parts of the learning process of infants occur due to chance. For example, the child happens to hit an object which is hanging over the bed when he/she is moving his/her arms around. If this occurs a sufficient number of times the child will develop an association between its own movement and the effect of this movement. A long time after the association has become established, the child will become conscious of it.

Give the child numerous opportunities to make chance discoveries of various kinds. Attach objects to a strong piece of elastic over the child's bed, or other places where the child spends time. Use objects you have at home and strong sticky tape or a piece of string. Do remember that objects which make noises are preferable to those which do not make any noise.

Some suggestions: Brightly-coloured wide sticky tape, wooden spoons, ribbons and plastic strings with attached bells, a small container made of metal with a stone inside, an empty toilet roll containing dried peas.

The next time the child is due for a present, think about getting a musical box.

WEEK 4

1   Continue to work on rhythm stimulation in the same way as last week. Vary the sounds (for example 'pa', 'tu', 'be').

2   The body massage is perhaps beginning to become a routine by now?

3   Continue to stimulate the child's ability to track a light beam or an object with his/her eyes in the same way as last week.

4   Make a bell bracelet for your child. Buy bells and sew them onto a piece of elastic. Put the bracelet alternately around the child's wrists and ankles. When the child moves his/her arms or legs the bells will make a sound. This is another chance behaviour you make use of.

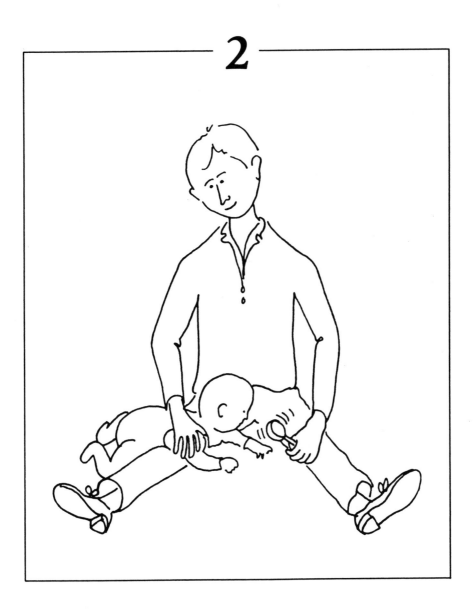

WEEK 1

1 The stimulation of rhythms will become more complicated from now on because you will be combining two syllables to one unit – one word. Say the following 'word' many times every day:

' dādā '

That is, two clear syllables of equal length joined together to make one word. To get the right form of the word you should repeat the word 'Daddy' to yourself as slowly as possible. Use this pronunciation as a model for how to say 'dada'.

2 Rhythmic body massage is a part of the programme every week. Since the massage of the body parts is carried out in the same order every time, the child will gradually develop an expectation of which body part will be massaged next. This is good.

3 **Goal:** For the child to track the vertical movement of an object.

Material: various things the child likes to look at. Try the following:

- Move an interesting object into the child's field of view. Make sure the child is watching the object.

- Move the object alternately upwards and downwards. Gradually increase the length of the movement from the starting point.

- If the child is not eye tracking, hold the child's chin and carefully move the head of the child upwards or downwards to follow the object.

- When the movement is completed, help the child to grasp the object with his/her own hands and move the object to the child's mouth.

Vary the child's position during this activity. Let the child lie on his/her back or sit on your lap.

4   The child's ability to listen needs to be stimulated so he/she gradually starts to look for where the sound is coming from.
     This is what you can do:

- collect together objects with different sounds, such as cellophane paper, two wooden spoons which can be banged together, a clock with a ticking sound, a bell, sound toys (but do not use toys with very loud, squeaky noises) and your own voice, of course.

- Make a sound with the objects you have collected (one at a time) just to the left and the right of the child's face. Make the sound close to the child's face. It is important that the child can see what you are doing.

- The child is probably looking at your face. Since you want the child to watch the object you are holding in your hand, you have to encourage the child to change his/her focus of vision. Move the bell into the child's field of vision. Then move the bell in the way shown in the pictures. Make sure the child's eyes are following the bell.

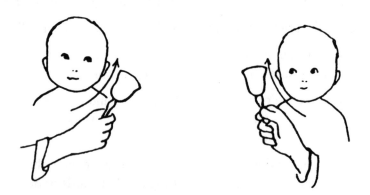

Try to find objects which the child seems to be interested in. Help the child every time to use his/her hands and mouth to explore the objects you are using during this and other activities!

WEEK 2

1   This week you should be saying the following 'word':

' dădă '

that is, two equally short syllables which forms a word. Pronounce
the word 'Daddy' as fast as you can. Use this pronunciation as a model
for how to say 'dada'.

2   Body massage. Rub the child's feet (hands) against each other in a
rhythmic way when the child is lying on the changing table. Let the
rhythm in this rubbing be the same as the rhythm of the sound
sequences the child is listening to in activity 1.

3   **Goal:** For the child to track an object's horizontal movement.

Material: Various interesting objects. Try using this 'doll': paint eyes,
nose and mouth with big black stokes on a piece of round, white
cardboard. Attach the cardboard to a stick.

Carry out the activity in the same way as activity 2 last week, but the
objects are moved from the centre to the sides instead of up and down.

4   **Goal:** For the child to search for a sound source with his/her gaze.

Material: The same objects which were used in activity 4 last week. The sounds should be known to the child.

This is what you do:

- The child is sitting on your lap. Make a well known sound close to the child's right ear. The child should not see what you are doing. .

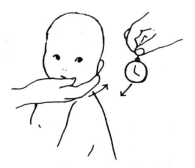

- If the child does not turn his/her head around towards the sound source, then carefully move the child's chin just a tiny bit in the right direction. Move the object into the child's field of view. Help the child hold the object and move it to his/her mouth.

Change ear and object.

Remember to complete the whole sequence from the sound to the child's attempt to touch and taste the object.

WEEK 3

1   When the child is listening to you, you may notice that the child is somehow quiet for a moment. This can be observed – the child's movements stop, the facial expression becomes calm and the eye gaze seems to be frozen. Learn to recognise these signals in your child.

This week the child should listen many times every day to the following rhythm variation:

' dādā,...dădă,...dādā,...dădă,... '

You start by saying the 'word' with the very long syllables. Repeat this word until you are sure that the child is listening to you. Then you change to the 'word' with the very short syllables. Repeat this word until you are sure that the child is listening. Then you change back to the first word again. Continue in this way as long as the child is paying attention.

2   Body massage. Continue rhythmic 'rubbing' of feet and hands.

3   **Goal:** For the child to track an object when lying on his/her stomach.

Material: a firmly rolled bath towel.
    Try this activity as an experiment. Leave the activity for a while if the child does not yet manage this position.
    This is what to do:

- Put the firmly rolled towel underneath the chest of the child with the child's arms over the roll. This position will support the child to keep his/her head and chest up from the floor.

- When the child is managing this position move an interesting object into the child's field of view.

- When the child is fixing his/her gaze on the object then move the object slightly higher.

- Keep the object in the high position and encourage the child to fix his/her eyes on the object for as long as possible.

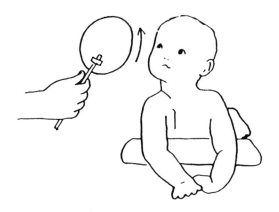

- When the child stops looking at the object, help him/her to investigate the object with his/her hands and mouth. Massage the shoulders of the child as well.

4   Repeat this activity in the same manner as activity 4 was carried out last week.

5   The child begins to discover the surrounding world more and more. These discoveries are often made when the child is carried around with or without a baby carrier. Remember to vary the way you are carrying your child. The most common way is perhaps to let the child's body lean against your chest with the child's face turned towards your own chest. Vary the carrying like this:

- Turn the child around sometimes so that the child's back is leaning against your chest.

- Let the chest of the child lean against your shoulder. In this position the child is encouraged to lift his/her head up and look around.

WEEK 4

1   This week give the child a third common word structure. This means that very many times every day you should say the 'word':

$$\text{`dādǎ'}$$

that is, the first syllable is very long and the second syllable is very short. To get the right form of this word you pronounce the word 'daughter' clearly and in an exaggerated way. Then use this pronunciation as a model for the word.

2   Body massage. 'Rubbing'.

3   Continue with the activity from last week, but move the object to the sides instead of upwards.

4 If the child is beginning to search for a sound source with his/her eyes as in activity 4 last week, expand the activity in the way which is described below. If the child does not search for the sound source with his/her eyes, then continue in the same way as described in week 2.

The activity could be carried out like this:

- Put the child on one side. Put one of your hands behind the child's back as a support.

- Move a well-known object into the child's field of view.

- When the child is fixing his/her eyes on the object, then move the object towards the child's ear that is facing upwards. Make a noise with the object.

- If the child does not move his/her face towards the sound source, help by turning the child to lie on his/her back using the hand you are holding on the child's back.

- When the child is lying on its back then the object is visible again to the child.

- You should of course help the child to grasp the object with his/her hands and move it to his/her mouth.

Vary the side on which the child is lying.

This activity can be the beginning of the child's ability to move from lying on the stomach to lying on the back and vice versa. However, do not expect your child to be able to do this for a long time yet. But stimulate your child often to look for a sound source in the way described above.

3

WEEK 1

Try to get a conversation going with the child. Pay attention to the child's signals.

If the child is seeking your eyes then you should interpret this as an invitation for communication; that is, the child is initiating a 'conversation' with you. Talk to the child while keeping eye contact. When you stop talking you may notice that the child is answering you with lively body movements. The child has 'said' his/her bit when his/her body movements quieten down. Take this as a signal that it is your turn to answer by talking to the child.

Try to communicate with your child on many occasions using this type of turn taking. Sometimes you take the initiative and at other times the child takes the initiative. What is important is that you pay attention to the signals of the child. You can perceive the child's conversation signals in his/her eye contact, facial expressions, body movements and sounds.

1   This week the child should hear the following sounds many times a day:

$$\text{dādā,...dādǎ,...dādā,...dādǎ,...}$$

Start by saying the word with equally long (very long). syllables. Repeat this word until you are sure the child is listening to you. Then change to the word with the same stress as in 'daughter' and repeat it until you are sure that the child is listening. Then change to the first word again. Continue in this manner as long as the child is paying attention.

2   A lot of stimulation can take place when the child is lying on the changing table. If the child is only wearing a few items of clothing the stimulation will be more effective.

Try the following:

- Press the palm of the child's hand against your own, rub the child's hands against each other. Play with the child's fingers one by one, straighten out and curl up the fingers. Press the child's finger tips against your own hand, relax – press... Move the arms of the child to the sides of his/her body and raise them up.

- Perform the same activities with the child's feet, toes and legs.

- Help the child to touch and feel his/her own feet using his/her hands. Move the child's big toe towards his/her mouth.

- Touch and tickle the child's body often. Play this game using a nursery rhyme, for example, 'Round and round the garden'.

Use your fingers and let them run over the child's body starting at the toes, running up the leg and over the chest and then tickle under the chin. If you carry out this activity in the same manner each time, the child will start to develop an expectation of what is going to happen next. This is good. Try to be very rhythmic both regarding your speech and your movements.

3 **Aim:** To follow a circular movement with the eyes.

The child is sitting on your lap. You are working on stimulating the child to follow an object with his/her eyes as you were doing earlier on. The difference this week is that you use a circular movement of the object.

As with all activities it is useful to increase the complexity of the activity, making it slightly harder for the child to carry out the activity. Adjust the activity to the child, ensuring that the activity is neither too easy nor too difficult. For the stimulation of vision the child is expected to be able to follow the movement of an object during an increasingly longer period of time. The movements are also being made larger, that is, moving further away from the starting point.

4   It is important to let the child experience many different sorts of movements, changes in position and posture. Try the following:

- Sit down on the floor with stretched out legs.

- Put the child over your legs close to your body which makes the child feel secure.

- Rock the child from side to side by moving first one leg and then the other. Adapt the size of the movements according to the child's ability to take part.

Carry out all these kinds of movements in a rhythmic way. Use this week's sounds together with this activity. This means that you are keeping the pace of the sounds with the pace of the movements of your legs. You say 'dada' with equally long and strong syllables at the same time as your right leg is moving in exactly the same manner as your left leg just did. When you move on to saying 'dada' with the first syllable long and strong while the second syllable is short and weaker then you move your left leg slowly and your right leg fast.

You can of course rock the child in your arms in a similar way. Or rock the child when he/she is lying on top of a big bed, using your hands.

There are all sorts of variations which you can use. Whatever you do, do not forget the rhythm.

Talk and sing to the child as often as possible. Always take the opportunity to **answer** the child's own sounds. This is a game, where you are learning to say the child's sounds. This is an important activity since the child will have his/her own sounds reinforced.

WEEK 2

1   The child will learn to recognise another important word structure in English. You should say the following word repeatedly every day:

dǎdā

that is, the first syllable is very short and the second syllable is very long. To find the right stress you should say the word 'before' very clearly. Use this as a model for the word.

2   A suitable material is needed when the child is starting to lie on the floor. One suggestion, if you are handy is to make a 'feely blanket', which the child can enjoy for a long time:

Take an old blanket and sew on pieces of material. The pieces should vary in shape, size, structure and colour. Do not attach all the pieces on all sides. Some pieces may be attached like pocket flaps. A button sewn on **securely** may be found underneath some flaps. Some pieces may be quilted, which will make them stand up a bit from the surface.

3   Continue to stimulate the child to follow different objects with the eyes. This may take place when the child is lying on its back, on its side or on its stomach; when the child is sitting on your lap, in a bouncing cradle (if he/she is using one) or in a baby carrier; when the child is carried both facing forwards and backwards and also when the child is standing on his/her legs (if the child is standing). Use various types of movements, for example, vertical, horizontal, circular and movements that go from the left side of the child all the way to the right side of the child and vice versa.

Look to see whether it is easier for the child to follow some types of movements. If, for instance, the child is showing difficulties in tracking an object moving to the left then you should of course give the child extra stimulation in tracking objects to the left.

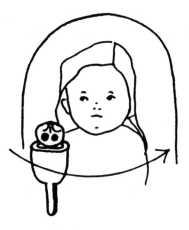

4   **Goal:** For the child to look towards a sound source.

Material: bath towel

various sound-making objects

someone to assist you

This activity is similar to what you have been doing earlier on. However, this activity is more difficult since another type of body movement is needed. Try the following: (Check with the Physiotherapist first)

- Put the child on its back on a bath towel which is placed on a bed or other soft surface.

- Make a sound next to the child's right ear.

- You should help the child to turn towards the sound source while the child can still hear the sound. One side of the towel can be lifted slightly, to make the child turn over. Adjust the movement to suit the child. It is not necessary to use a bath towel when you help the child to turn. You can turn the child onto his/her side by placing your hands directly on the child's hips and turning the hips.

- As soon as the child has changed position, let him/her hear the sound again and see the object. Help the child to explore the object with hands and mouth.

- Change to the other ear so that the child is moving towards the right side the first time and towards the left side the second time.

WEEK 3

1   This week the child should hear the following sounds many times over each day:

dădă,...dādă,...dădă

Start off by saying the word with the very short (equally short) syllables. Repeat this until you feel sure that the child is listening. Then change to the word which sounds like 'daughter' and repeat this until you see that the child is listening. Then change again. Continue like this as long as the child is paying attention.

2   It is very useful to know a number of nursery rhymes. You may vary the rhyme from last week as you stimulate the back of the child's body:
Run your fingers from the heels, along the legs and over the buttocks and back and finally tickle the back of the neck.

3   Continue the stimulation of vision in the same way as last week.

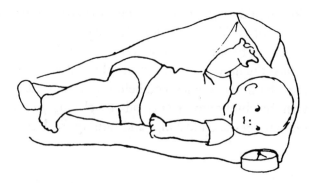

4   Perform this activity in the same manner as last week with one
    exception. Place the child on its stomach on the towel and turn the
    child to each side and over to his/her back using the towel.

WEEK 4

1   This week the child should listen to the following sound sequence
    many times over every day:

dădā,...dādă,...dădā,...

Start by saying the word which has the same stress as 'before'. Repeat
this word until you feel sure that the child is listening. Then swap to
the word which has the same stress as 'daughter' and repeat this word
as many times as is necessary for the child to listen to it. Then swap
again. Continue like this many times over.

2   This activity is carried out in the same way as last week.

3   This activity is carried out in the same way as last week.

4   During this activity, the child is looking towards the sound source by
    rolling over. The child may find the rolling over unpleasant. Does the
    child start to put his/her hands out to take the fall?

5   Shortly we will start to introduce activities which stimulate grasping.
    The development of motor skills of the hands and grasping play an
    important part in the child's adjustment to the surrounding world. It
    is therefore important to stimulate the child's interest and skill to use
    his/her hands in a functional manner from an early age.
    Here are a few suggestions for stimulation:

    • Attach buttons or empty cotton reels of different shapes and
      sizes to a strong string. The objects can be spaced out by
      making knots on the string. This is now a 'feely string' for
      the child.

- There are plenty of different sorts of brushes for sale. Give the child a selection of brushes to play with.

- Velcro is also something which can be used in various different ways. Find two ribbons. Sew a piece of Velcro onto each ribbon. Attach the ribbons to the child's hands. The child will need to use some strength to pull the hands apart. Of course you play this game together with the child and help the child to move his/her hands apart.

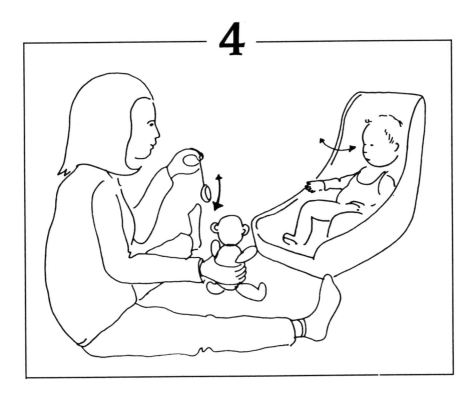

4

WEEK 1

1 Make use of every opportunity to stimulate the child's 'conversational' skills. When you observe your child closely, you will probably notice that the child knows the basic rules of a conversation. When you talk to the child and are engaging in eye contact, the child is quiet and calm, but when you stop talking and listen for an answer, he/she will become more lively and make sounds.

Continue to develop this skill by imitating the child's sounds and movements as closely as possible. In addition, try to prolong your conversation **but** be aware that the child will finish the conversation by turning away his/her eyes.

Remember that eye contact is the be all and end all in this activity. It is **impossible** to carry out this activity too many times. You can try the following:

- When you have established eye contact then you say 'aaaaa'. Or perhaps the child initiates the eye contact and says something or moves.

- Copy the child's sounds, movements and facial expressions.

- The child talks again and you imitate.

Let the child direct the conversation this week.

2   The visual stimulation continues.

Goal: For the child to move his/her eyes from one toy to another.

Material: All sorts of objects of different form, colour and size. Only use two objects at a time.

Let the child either sit up or lie down while you carry out this activity. Sometimes sitting, sometimes lying down. Make sure there are no distracting objects in the child's view.

Try the following:

- Show one toy to the child, that is, move one toy into the child's field of view. Make sure the child is looking at the object.

- Then bring the other toy into the child's field of view.

- Put the objects in front of the child if he/she is sitting up. Attach the toys to a string using pegs if the child is lying down.

- When the child has looked at both objects, help him/her to explore the toys one at a time. Help the child to grasp the toy and move it towards his/her mouth for further exploration.

- Finally, help the child to move his/her hands together right in front of his/her body.

The next time you carry out this activity, show **both** toys to the child at the same time. Check carefully whether the child is moving his/her eyes from one object to the other and back again. If this does not occur, then follow the same procedure as you used during the first activity, that is, 'showing' one toy at a time.

Use a variety of toys and other objects. Move the toy into the child's view slowly on some occasions and quickly on others.

Always make sure the child can see, feel and taste the toys/objects every time.

3   Encourage the child's own initiatives in all sorts of situations. Here is one example:

Goal: For the child to intensify his/her kicking.

Material: Various sound toys.

The child is lying on his/her back in a place where you can attach a string at a suitable kicking height. Attach **one** toy to the string. The toy should make a noise when kicked quite lightly.

Initially, the child will kick the toy just by chance. To develop kicking more quickly in this situation, you can help the child to make further kicks by holding his/her leg and assisting another kick – the toy makes a noise –... another kick – the toy makes a noise...

Encourage kicks with the right leg, left leg and both legs together.

4   Body massage, finger and toe stimulation.

Idea:

A trampoline can be fun for the whole family. A trampoline could already now be a very positive experience for your young child and a good investment for the future.

Of course your child cannot jump on the trampoline yet but he/she can lie on it and at a later stage sit on it. When the child is lying on the trampoline his/her sounds and movements will be amplified in a way that does not happen when he/she is lying on a blanket on the floor. The child's movements and sounds are intensified by the trampoline and this stimulates the child's body. Initially, unintentional movements will be intensified. After some time they will become conscious, intentional movements.

There are different sorts of trampolines available. Choose one that gives good resonance and is elastic enough to cause vibrations even with small movements.

WEEK 2

1   Continue to 'converse' with the child. Perhaps you would like to start to play around with different sounds to see if the child reacts to the way you sound.

Continue to imitate the sounds the child makes in the same way as last week with just one change. Answer the child with a rising tone. Start in your normal tone of voice (which you usually use when you talk) and at the end raise your tone of voice to a high tone, for example:

' aaaaa '

Do, exaggerate!

This game with the rising pitch is to an extent a continuation of the previous sound activities you have carried out. You may have noticed that the child does react to long and short sound sequences. The thought behind the current activity is similar: by 'bombarding' the child with exaggerated pitch variations the child will also start to recognise and react to these.

2 The visual stimulation continues from last week, but you now use three toys. The goal is for the child to switch his/her attention between three different toys. Work in the same manner as last week.

3 Continue the kicking in the same way as last week. Perhaps you have noticed that the child can kick several times in a row and/or kick harder???

4 Body massage, finger and toe stimulation.

WEEK 3

1 Continue to converse in the same way as during week 2, with the only difference that you answer the child with a falling tone.

' aaaaaa '

Start on your normal tone and make the tone fall to a lower tone at the end.

2   The visual stimulation continues in the same manner as last week if necessary. Yet another skill is to be stimulated.

Goal: The child is to track a vertical movement – slow upward movement and fast downward movement as an object is dropped.

The child is sitting in your lap at a table – there should be a short distance between the highest and lowest falling point.

- Show the child an interesting object, perhaps a small paper plate covered with aluminium foil, which reflects sounds.

- When the child is looking at the object, it is slowly moved upwards. The child needs to track the movement with his/her eyes.

- Hold the object just above the child's nose. The child should be looking at the object.

- Drop the object.

- The child will probably not look at the falling object which will land on the table. 'Show' the object again, that is, see – feel – taste and repeat the activity.

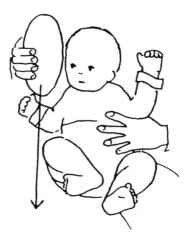

Use different sorts of objects. A big balloon may be easy to start off with since it falls slowly. Let the object fall down sometimes on the right, sometimes to the left and sometimes straight in front of the child. It is best if the objects make a noise when they fall.

3   **Goal:** The child kicks sound toys from a sitting position (on the lap).

Material: Sound toys which won't fall when kicked.

The child will probably need much more help to be able to kick when sitting compared to lying down.

WEEK 4

1   Continue to converse with the child. Play around with rising and falling tones. Also vary the way in which you copy the child's sounds sometimes using short sounds and sometimes using long sounds. Remember to exaggerate the tone variations. Does the child seem to enjoy your 'chats'? Are the child's sounds at all influenced by the way you sound?

Make use of opportunities to talk often to the child. Use all your imagination and expression. Try to read messages in the child's expressions. Try to imagine what the child could possibly want to try to say. One example: If the child makes a sound and a movement and you see a doll in the child's field of view, you could say 'Do you want the doll?' And then you give the child the doll.

2   Another variation of the visual stimulation will be added this week. The activity is also a preparation for playing peekaboo.

Goal: For the child to track an object's horizontal movement, even if the whole movement is not visible.

Use very interesting objects for this activity, for example, which is shining towards the child's face. Try the following: 'show' the child the object. When the child is looking at the object, move the object to the right. A part of the movement can be obscured by the leg of a chair, a tea cup, or a thermos. However, the object should never come to rest while it is out of the child's view.

If the child stops tracking the object, that is, does not look at the place where the object appears again, then stop the movement and let the child see, feel and taste the object. Change to the left side and vary the objects.

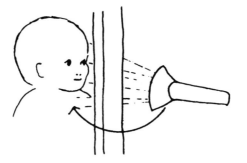

3   Continue as suggested last week.

4   Continue as suggested last week.

5

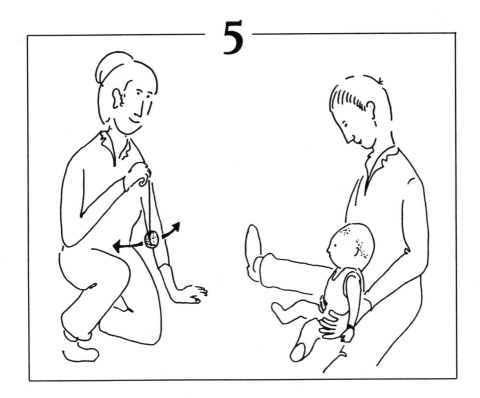

WEEK 1

1   Various theories of language development suggest that babbling and speech are related to one another. There seems to be a continuous development from babbling to speech which depends, among other things, on the child's motor development and hearing. The babbling child is making itself ready for speech. The development of babbling goes through several stages which are more or less the same for most children. There is an order in which the child starts to use sound sequences. This is the reason why you should stimulate babbling. The stimulation will continue for a long period of time and it will become more complex as time goes on.

Do not feel restricted by the suggestions you will be given. They will suit some parents but not all. Try to use the suggestions in a manner that suits you and your child.

Play with sounds – long and short, loud and quiet, common and uncommon.

Play with 'melodies' and tone variations when you are talking.

Always let your facial expression and body movements reflect what you are saying.

It is of course important that you and your child are having a dialogue – that you are quiet and wait for the child to reply and that you answer the child when he/she has spoken.

You say	*The child says*
ab a	something
abab a	something
ababab a	something

Your 'conversations' could look like this (at least a few times every day):
continue for as long as you like.

The boxed in ⊡a⊡ indicates that the vowel should be long, stressed and have a rising tone.

Your child probably has difficulty in hearing the difference between various sounds (especially between some sounds). By 'bombarding' the child with certain sound sequences the child will learn to recognise different sound patterns. The child's interest for sounds is then expected to increase.

As soon as you have found a form for these structured conversations which suits you, observe carefully how the child answers you. Continue to 'mirror' each other as much as possible. This means that you might answer the child with, for example, 'ababababa' if the child makes a long sound, but with 'aba' if the child makes a short sound. If you enjoy these conversations then you will gradually develop a sensitivity for 'mirroring'. You will answer the child with exactly the same number of syllables as the child says without thinking about it.

2   During the coming weeks the visual stimulation will be co-ordinated with the development of hand function.

Goal: For the child to track an object's vertical movement from low to high.

Material: Objects with different feel and sounds, for example a rattle on a string, a big plastic flower on a string or a soft plastic ball on a string.

Start this activity by trying to make the child look at his/her own hands.

Proceed as follows:

- Place the child in front of you, sitting on another adult's lap or propped up with cushions (depending on the child's ability to sit). **Never** give more support than is necessary. Do not support the child's upper back, if he/she can manage to sit with support at his/her waist. Alternatively, put the child on his/her stomach with a rolled towel supporting his/her chest (with the purpose of making the child lift his/her head and raise his/her arms).

- Hold an object in front of the child; say 'Look, a ball' (or whatever). Move the object slightly.

- If the child does not reach spontaneously for the object, take the child's hands and help him/her to touch the object.

- When you are sure that the child is looking at the moving object, move it upwards. The child should follow the movement with his/her eyes and head. At the same time as you are raising the object, say or sing 'ba,ba,ba,**baaaa**' (holding the object still). Use the same sound sequence as described in activity one.

- If the child stops looking at the moving object, then stop and repeat from the start.

- **Praise** each of the child's attempts to track the object. Give the object to the child. It is important for the child to see, feel and taste the object. But it is also starting to become important for the child to explore objects with his/her hands. Together you will shake the rattle, squeeze the ball, and so on.

You might like to massage the child's hands by making movements so the child's wrists have to make circular movements.

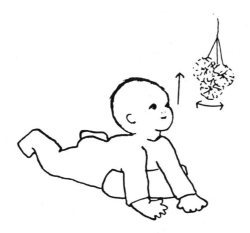

3   Here is a routine game which may be played on the changing table for some time to come:

Play peekaboo like this:

- Hide your eyes, putting one hand over your eyes – 'Where is Mummy/Daddy?'

- Take away your hand – eye contact – 'Peekaboo'

- Place a tissue over half of your face – 'Where is Mummy/Daddy?'

- Take away the tissue – eye contact – 'Peekaboo'.

Remember to hide your face when the child is looking at you.
Later on it will be the child's turn to hide him/herself in the same manner.

- One hand over the child's eyes...

- A tissue over half of the child's face...etc...

4   Has the child started to roll over on his/her own initiative yet?

Rolling from side to back or stomach?

Rolling from back or stomach to side?

Rolling from stomach to back?

If this has not started to happen yet then it may be time to help the child gradually to experience the movements involved. The Physiotherapist can advise you.

5   Continue the body massage.

6   It is very important that you are using gestures and facial expression when you talk to your child. It may feel unnatural to start off with, but remember that we all use gestures often.

This month's gestures:

- 'Come' – **outstretched arms** towards the child at the same time as you are saying come.

- 'Look' – **pointing** from your eyes towards what you want the child to look at.

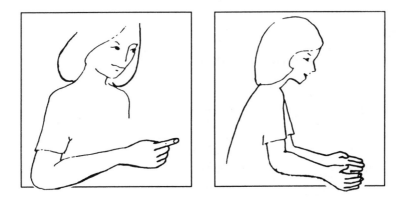

Always use these gestures from today onwards.

WEEK 2

1   The structured conversation this week looks like this:

Eye contact

You say	The child says
ab a	something
ab a ba	something
abab a b a	something

repeat from the start as many times as you want.

2   This activity is carried out in the same manner as last week.

3   This activity is carried out in the same manner as last week.

4   This activity is carried out in the same manner as last week.

5   This activity is carried out in the same manner as last week.

6   This activity is carried out in the same manner as last week.
    Has the child started to become interested in mirrors? Perhaps it
is time to let the child look into a mirror more often.

WEEK 3

1   This week's structured conversation:

Eye contact

You say	The child says
awa	something
awawa	something
awawawa	something

2   The visual stimu-
    lation continues in
    almost the same
    manner as in week
    1, but the child
    should track an
    object moving
    sideways. Gradu-
    ally increase the
    object's move-
    ments so that in
    the end the child
    needs to turn the

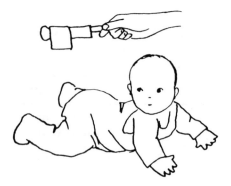

upper part of the his/her body to follow the object.

Remember to give the child the object to explore at the end of every activity. Give the object sometimes from the left, sometimes from the right. When the child has grasped the object, help him/her to move his/her hands forward in front of his/her body.

Do not give up this activity if the child finds it hard to turn the upper part of his/her body. On the contrary, pay extra attention to the activities which demand some sort of rotation of a part of the body. Many children need a lot of stimulation to be able to carry out these activities.

3   This activity is carried out in the same manner as during week 1.

4   This activity is carried out in the same manner as during week 1.

5   This activity is carried out in the same manner as during week 1.

6   This activity is carried out in the same manner as during week 1.

7   A little bit of extra time this week can be spent on the child's feet. Help the child to grasp a foot, or both feet (if the arms can reach) and rock the child gently. Put the child's toes into his/her mouth.

The following nursery rhyme makes the stimulation of the child's toes easier.

Touch one toe at a time, wiggle it, blow on it...

THIS LITTLE PIGGY
This little piggy (big toe) went to market,
this little piggy stayed at home,
this little piggy ate roast beef,
this little piggy had none,
this little piggy went wee, wee, wee, **all** the way home.

WEEK 4

1   This week's structured conversation looks like this:

Eye contact

You say	*The child says*
aba	something
ababa	something
abababa	something
awa	something
awawa	something
awawawa	something

Vary this sequence occasionally by stressing the second vowel instead of the last vowel.

2   Continue the activity in the same way as last week. The activity can be carried out using a bottle as a signal for the child to have a drink. When the child has reached for the bottle, help the child to hold his/her hand around it as he/she is drinking.

   This activity could take place every time the child drinks from the bottle in the future.

3   This activity is carried out in the same manner as last week.

4   This activity is carried out in the same manner as last week.

5   This activity is carried out in the same manner as last week.

6   This activity is carried out in the same manner as last week.

7   There are plenty of opportunities for finger – and toe – rhymes.
     Generally children like rhymes, perhaps because they have a rhythm
     and are repeated in the same way every time. There are many books
     at the library with old and new rhymes for all sorts of occasions.
     Falling asleep rhymes, eating rhymes, rhymes for their own sake, and
     so on.
         Here is a common rhyme. Start with clenched fist and pop up each
     of the child's fingers as it is 'called'. Massage each finger one at a time.
     Speak clearly and with a distinct rhythm.

     Tommy Thumb, Tommy Thumb, where are you?
     Here I am, here I am, how do you do?

     Peter Pointer, Peter Pointer, where are you?
     Here I am, here I am, how do you do?

     Toby Tall, Toby Tall…etc

     Ruby Ring, Ruby Ring…etc

     Baby Small, Baby Small…etc.

6

WEEK 1

1 The structured conversations continue for some time. The conversation for this week looks like this:

Eye contact

You say	*The child says*
obo	xxxxxx
obobo	xxxxxx
obobobo	xxxxxx
obobo	xxxxxx
obobobo	xxxxxx

Repeat these sequences and occasionally use the 'aba' – sequences. Also vary the stress so that different vowels are stressed. Play with the child's lips during these conversations.

2 **Goal:** For the child to stop whatever he/she is doing and to look towards the sound source. For this activity you will need someone to assist you.

Try the following:

- Put the child on your lap. Together you should bang toys against each other or on the table or perhaps just explore the toys by turning them. Make sure the child is paying attention to what you are doing.

- Another adult should say the child's name several times using an interesting voice.

- If the child does not look up to locate the calling voice with his/her eyes, then you should help the child by gently turning his/her face towards the talking person.

- Hopefully, the child is pleased to see who is calling.

3   This is a play activity which you probably will spend quite some time on during months to come. You may not always realise that you are in fact playing this game, since it is many children's favourite game: The 'take – and – give' – game.

     This week we'll be starting with the first part of the game: 'Take'.

Goal: For the child to look at, reach out for and pick up an object.

Material: Collect in a basket or bag a number of objects of different appearance, feel and taste. Use a mix of objects well known to the child and new objects.

Try the following:

- Show the child a toy.

- Move the object forward a little bit, say 'Take...for example dolly' at the same time as you make *the gesture* for '*to take*' (a grasping hand movement in the air).

Always use this gesture from now on when you say 'take...'.

- If the child does not do what you want, then help by making sure the child is looking at the object. Then pick up the object together while holding the child's hands.

4   **Goal:** For the child to lift his/her head and if possible chest from the floor by supporting him/herself on outstretched arms.

Try the following:

- The child is lying on his/her stomach on the floor or on a trampoline.

- Make a noise with a toy above the child's head slightly to one side.

- If the child does not spontaneously lift his/her head and chest up to look at the object, then help by putting your hand under the child's chest and gently lifting the chest slightly.

- Try to keep the child's attention for longer periods of time. The child then has to support him/herself on outstretched arms for longer periods of time.

- When you reckon it is time to stop, give the child the toy and help him/her to explore it.

- As soon as possible try to encourage the child to let one hand go and reach for the toy, while the other hand is supporting and balancing the body. This is probably

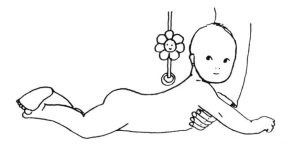

something the child cannot manage yet, but persist with this activity until the child can manage. Remember to hand the toys to the child from all directions: from above and underneath, from the sides as well as from in front of the child. It is very important for the child to learn to estimate the distance by using his/her hands in all directions.

5   Massage. Be more specific by saying the name of each body part when you are giving the massage.

WEEK 2

1   The structured conversation for this week looks like this:

Eye contact

You say	The child says
awa	xxxxxx
awawa	xxxxxx
awawawa	xxxxxx

Repeat these sequences. Vary the stress of vowels. Also vary by saying 'owo' –, 'aba' –, and 'obo' – sequences, but use 'awa' most of the time.

As before listen carefully to the child's own sounds. If the child is making a sound similar to an 'a', then answer with 'awa' – or 'aba' – sequences. *Don't forget to mirror the child's sounds with your own speech.*

2   Continue with the activity in the same manner as last week but make sure the voice is coming from different places and distances in the room.

3   Continue with the 'Take' game. Change the objects frequently; toothbrushes, spoons and similar things are easy to pick up. Remember to help the child each time by exploring the object by banging the object against the table, brushing it on the knee, or banging it gently against the chest.

4   When the child can manage to support him/herself on outstretched arms and look around then try to encourage the child to move on his/her stomach around his/her own axis like the hands on a clock. The trampoline is a good surface for this activity.

Material: Different objects hanging from strings.

Try the following:

- Show the child the object, point and say (for example) 'Look! a car'.

- When the child is looking at the object, slowly pull the object towards the right or left (change sides). Only move the object a little bit to start off with so the child is able to follow the movement.

- Little by little extend the movement so the child has to turn his/her head and upper part of the body to follow the whole movement. The child will gradually start to move his/her hands sideways and kick backwards with the legs and in that manner move round on his/her stomach.

- Every time you have triggered a movement with an object, complete and finish by letting the child explore the object. This should take place regardless of how long the child was able to track the object.

5   Massage.

6   Start collecting various different materials for a feely book. The book is an introduction to reading books but foremost an activity to stimulate the fingers. Make the book by gluing/sewing different materials onto pages in a scrap-book.

The pages of the book do not need to look like anything in particular, what is important is that the materials feel different from each other, when the child's fingers move over the pages. For example, you could make a pattern using velvet and sandpaper on one page. Use your imagination and things you have at home for the book.

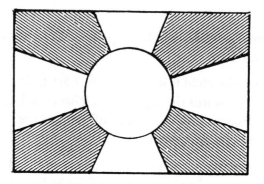

WEEK 3

1   The structured conversation for this week:
repeat and vary in the same way as last week.

You say	*The child says*
ada	xxxxxx
adada	xxxxxx
adadada	xxxxxx

2   The activity should be carried out in a similar manner to week 1. You do not need another person to assist you now – leave the child to sit and play on his/her own. Say the child's name. Also try this behind the child's back. It is important that the child looks at you every time his/her name is called without any physical help.

3   This week's 'Take' game can be made more advanced by putting the object that is to be picked up on a string which is hanging from a vertical elastic band. A wooden ring with an attached bell or a rattle is suitable.

What happens when the child takes the object?

When the child is pulling the ring (or the rattle) a sound is made and the ring and the elastic band move. When the child lets go of the object the movements of the object and the elastic band are exaggerated.

4   Continue the activity in the same way as last week. Change the objects often and gradually increase the size of the movement.

5   Massage.

WEEK 4

1   The structured conversation this week looks like this:

Eye contact

You say	The child says
aya	xxxxxx
ayaya	xxxxxx
ayayaya	xxxxxx

Also use 'aba'-, 'ava'–, 'ada' sequences. But make sure the child is 'bombarded' with 'aya'–sequences most of all.

Repeat the sequences to make them both long and short. **Remember:** *listen to the child.*

2   This activity is carried out in a similar manner to week 1, but instead of using your voice, use different objects that make sounds.

If the child does not react to the sound, that is, does not stop playing with a toy and does not look up to locate the sound, then help the child as before.

3 It is probably too early to add the 'Give' part to the 'Take-and-give' game but it may be worthwhile trying.

   Instead of you giving the child an object, it is now your turn to request the object that the child is holding in his/her hand. Say for example: 'Give me the spoon' at the same time as you make the gesture for '*Give me*': The palm of your hand reached forward towards the child in a distinct manner.

Always use this gesture from now on.

4 The activity of week 2 is continued. Carry on doing this activity until the child is able to move around in a circle on his/her stomach.

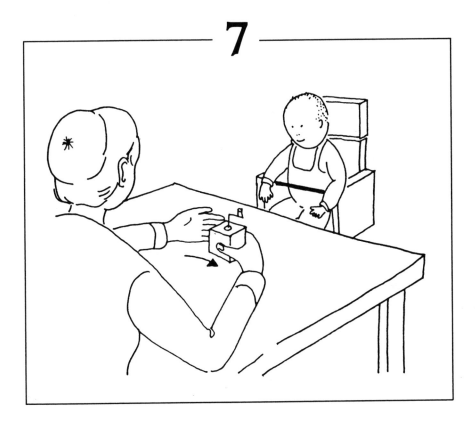

7

WEEK 1

1 The structured conversation this week looks like this:

'ibi' sequences

'iwi' sequences

'idi' sequences

'iyi' sequences

'Bombard' the child with these sound sequences. Record your conversations if you have a tape recorder at home. Let the child listen to the tape.

2 Continue the 'take and give' game. Here is a suggestion of how to make the game slightly more difficult. You need someone to help you carry out the activity.

The child is sitting on the table with his/her back against you. Support the child's hips. Make sure the child is not sitting with his/her legs too far apart.

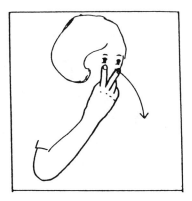

The third person should sit opposite the child.

- This person says, for example, 'Look...(the name of the child) a ball. Take the ball'. The gestures for 'look' and 'take' should be made at the same time as the words are spoken. **Always** use the child's name as a signal for the child to listen.

- The helper should then hold the ball in front of the child at a distance so that the child needs to reach forwards and **upwards** to get hold of the ball. Sometimes straight in front, sometimes to the left or right above the child.

- Make sure the activity is completed each time; that is, the child reaches for the toy with or without your help and explores it.

3   There will be various forms of hiding games to play over a long period of time. Of course it will take time for the child to fully understand each game. Since the game does not require a lot of preparation it can be played whenever you wish. Make a habit of trying the hiding games in all sorts of situations.

All you need to do is as follows:

- When the child is looking at the object you are showing – move it **slowly** towards one side and behind a juice carton, a toothbrush mug, a blanket, etc.

- After a moment – before the child has turned his/her eyes away from the object – bring the object out and give it to the child.

- Explore the object together by squeezing it, tearing it (if it is paper), banging it, shaking it, throwing it, pulling it...

4   Becoming aware of the fingers and what they can be used for is an important discovery for your child. Finger and hand rhymes are useful for this purpose. Try the following:

Two little dicky birds
Sitting on a wall
One named Peter
One named Paul
Fly away Peter
Fly away Paul
Come back Peter
Come back Paul

Pretend that your hands are the two birds which fly away and come back.

It is also important to stimulate different hand functions.

Goal: For the child to hold one object in each hand.

Material: Small objects that are easy to pick up, two of each sort, such as skipping rope handles, toothbrushes or pegs.

- Sit opposite the child. Hold two objects, one in each hand in front of the child's hands.

- Say 'take' at the same time as you move the objects towards the child's hands.

- If the child does not reach out for the objects, then help him/her. Put your hands on top of the child's small hands and together grasp and hold the object.

- As soon as the child can manage to hold the objects, play with them by banging them against each other in front of the child.

- The activity can be made more difficult if the objects are of different size.

5   Massage.

Massage the child's fingers starting at the fingertips and moving towards the wrist, both the inside and outside of the hand. Give each finger individual attention, stretch out and curl the fingers.

WEEK 2

1   The structured conversation this week looks like this:

'ebe' sequences

'ewe' sequences

'ede' sequences

'eye' sequences

2   This activity is to be carried out in the same manner as during week 1. The only difference is for the child to reach forwards and **downwards**.

The child may loose balance when he/she tries to reach for the object you are holding. If this happens, help the child to straighten up his/her body and regain balance. Make the activity more difficult by encouraging the child to reach further forwards.

Perhaps mechanical toys are starting to become exciting? There are many different sorts of toys which move when they are wound up. Look in the toy shop.

3   Continue the activity in the same way as last week.

The activity can be made more difficult by keeping the object hidden for longer periods of time. Always let the child see the object before he/she has lost interest.

4   **Goal:** For the child to hold a large object, when co-ordination of both hands is needed.

Material: Objects which are so big that the child cannot hold on with only one hand. Do not choose objects, which are too heavy try, for example, balloons, plastic balls or a relatively big saucepan with two handles.

Carry out the activity in a similar way to last week. Give the child the support needed. Help the child to hold on to the objects together with your hands on top of his/her hands if necessary.

5   Massage.

6   Does the child like to stand on your lap with his/her arms supported?

   If not, try to encourage this (check with the physiotherapist whether the child is ready for this activity). When you are helping the child to stand up in your lap, **always** use the gesture for up (lift your hands with palms up).

   Always use this gesture when you tell the child to stand up.

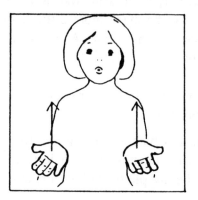

WEEK 3

1   The structured conversation this week:

   'ama' sequences

   'amo' sequences

   'omo' sequences

   'eme' sequences

   Listen to your child. Adjust your sounds to the sounds that the child is making.

2   Continue in the same manner as during week 1. Give the child the objects from the sides in such a way that the child needs to turn his/her trunk to reach.

Be persistent with this activity. The child may need a lot of stimulation to turn the trunk without the lower part of the body turning as well.

3   The hiding game can be varied this week:

- When you are sure the child is looking at the object, move it slowly down and put it in front of the child on a table or the floor.

- When the child is looking, take the child's hand and put it on top of the object and cover the child's hand with a handkerchief. If the child does not spontaneously pull his/her hand out while holding the object, then help the child by lifting off the handkerchief.

4   **Goal:** For the child to pick up and hold one object in each hand.

Material: Objects that are easy to grasp. Vary the object's form, texture, colour and weight.
Try the following:

- Sit opposite the child. Show the child a doll, for example, say: 'NN(the child's name), look, a doll. Take the doll', at the same time as making the gestures **look** and **take**.

- When the child is holding the doll and has explored it for a little while, show another object, for example, a car. Say 'NN, look a car, take the car' at the same time as you are making the gestures for **look** and **take**. Move the car close to the child's hands. Make this movement very obvious.

- In order to pick up the car the child may let go of the doll. Perhaps the child will drop the doll automatically.

- The purpose of this activity is for the child **not** to drop the doll. You may need to put one of your hands on top of the child's hand and together hold on to the doll while the car is picked up with the other hand. Put your other hand on top of the child's hand that is now holding on to the car.

- Now the child – with or without your help – is holding the doll in one hand and the car in the other.

5   Massage.

6   When the child is standing in your lap, a third person may encourage the child to look around by turning the upper part of the trunk (compare with activity no. 2).

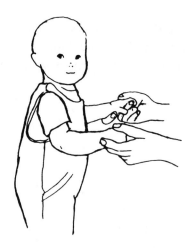

WEEK 4

1   The structured conversation this week:

'ababa' sequences

'ababo' sequences

'ababe' sequences

'ababi' sequences

Vary the length of the sequences. The child is probably capable of uttering rather long sound strings. If the child does, answer back in the same way. But always stress the last vowel, making it sound different from the other vowels.

2   This activity is to be a repeat of weeks 1,2 and 3. This means giving the child objects from above, in front and sometimes from the sides. During all activities it is useful for the child to reach as far as possible to be able to grasp the object. Is the child able to regain balance on his/her own?

   If the child has long arms, try to show the child how it feels to sit with support from his/her own arms.

3   This week the hiding game is developed into the game that your child may like the most of all the games:
   the 'throw everything on to the floor' game.

   • When the child is watching the object you are showing, drop it on the floor.

   • As soon as the child looks at the object, pick it up from the floor.

   • When the child has explored the object, ask to have it back by saying 'Give me...' at the same time as you make the **give me** gesture.

   • When you have been given the object, drop it on the floor again...and pick it up...and show it to the child...and start all over again.

4   Carry out the activity in the same manner as during last week.

5   Massage

6   It is already time to think about how the child is going to eat to plan for future eating patterns. As soon as possible, stop feeding the child only mashed food. As soon as possible the child should be introduced to drinking from a normal glass or cup. Do not use cups with lids, since the tongue easily gets into the wrong position when a lid is used. Remember the following:

- The child's eating should be **active**. This means a lot of things, for example making the child try to reach for the next spoonful. Encourage this by touching the lips and perhaps the tongue with the spoon, the moment before you put the spoon into the mouth.

- If the tongue comes out of the mouth, first push the tongue into the mouth using the spoon. Second, give the child the next spoonful of food.

- Small bits of food are placed at either side of the tongue, not in the middle of the tongue.

- When the child is drinking from a glass – make sure the rim of the glass is not resting on the child's tongue. Push the tongue inside the mouth before putting the glass to the lips.

- Let the child have his/her own spoon or at least hold one while you are feeding with another spoon, or preferably a fork.

8

WEEK 1

1   The structured conversation this week looks like this:

'abib' sequences

'abob' sequences

'abab' sequences

Has the child got a favourite sound? If this sound is very dominating then try not to reinforce it by answering with the same sound.

2   A lot of activities to come involve some imitation. The ability to imitate is probably vital for the child's development. This is why you should persist in trying to make the child imitate both sounds and movements.

Goal: For the child to imitate the gesture 'come' ('pick me up' gesture). Initially you will need a third person when you carry out the activity.

- Sit down with the child on your lap.

- The third person talks to the child and says 'come' while reaching his/her arms towards the child.

- Take the child's arms and make the same gesture with the child's arms.

- Now the child is making the same gesture as the adult and is picked up.

After some time you may only need to touch the child's arms slightly for the child to make the gesture.

Remember that the child's gesture – even if it is only a hint of a gesture – will end up with the desired result: the child is picked up.

3   The 'hiding' game and the 'hide and seek' game are combined in the following activity. Use all sorts of objects which can be hidden in your hand(s) for example keys, a spoon, a dummy, a watch.

- Give the child the object in the same way as in the 'take' game.

- Hide the object in your hands while the child is looking at your hand(s). Shake your hand(s) to keep the child's attention.

- Open your hand(s) and give the object to the child again and start the activity all over again.

- The child receives the object again and explores it. Allow the child time to use both hands while exploring the object by twisting and turning it right in front of the child's body.

4   Continue to stimulate and play with the child's hands and fingers. Here is a new finger rhyme:

This little cow eats grass,
This little cow eats hay,
This little cow looks over the hedge,
This little cow runs away.
And this **BIG** cow does nothing at all,

But lie in the fields all day.
We'll chase her,
And chase her,
And chase her!

For this finger-counting rhyme, start at the little finger and end by pouncing on the thumb.

Pointing and the use of the index fingers to explore objects are important features in the child's exploration of the environment.

A pointing book with raised objects may be useful now. Point to and feel the pictures using the index fingers.

It is easy to make a pointing book. Cut pictures out of various materials with different textures, for example sandpaper, cardboard, velvet. Some possible outlines are provided on the following pages. The pictures may be stuffed so that they clearly stand out from the page. Tie the pages together with a piece of string. This will enable you to expand the book with more pictures.

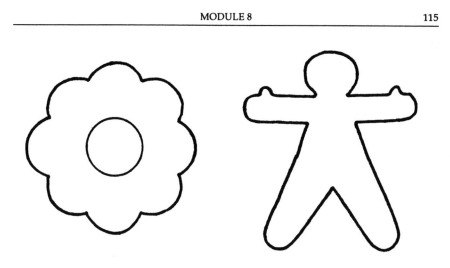

5   Encourage the child to turn around if the child is capable of sitting up without support. Make sure that the child is not sitting with the legs abnormally far apart. (Check with the physiotherapist whether the child is ready for this activity.)

    Use the same method as when you encouraged the child to turn around on his/her stomach.

6   Try various support positions if the child does not sit without support. Perhaps the child is able to sit up while supporting his/her arms on his/her own knees? Let the child experience as many different positions as possible.

7   Massage combined with naming of the different body parts.

WEEK 2

1   The structured conversation this week looks like this:

> alal
>
> alalal
>
> alalalal

Vary by changing the 'a' to an 'ee' or an 'o'. Also vary the length of the sequences.

Remember to **listen** to the child's sounds.

2   The imitation activity from last week continues. You probably need to carry on practising the 'pick me up' gesture.

Also work on waving 'hello' and 'bye-bye'. Help the child to imitate waving in the same way as you worked on the gesture 'pick me up'.

3   The 'hide' and the 'take' game is carried out in the same way as last week.

4   Carry out this activity in the same manner as last week.

5   It is desirable if the child starts to move over the floor of his/her own accord. The type of movement may, for example, be rolling or crawling. Try to make it as easy as possible for the child to move. The Physiotherapist may advise you how actively to assist the child's crawling.

When the child is lying on his/her stomach on the floor and tries to move forward without success – press the child's foot soles with your hands. When you feel that the child's legs are becoming more active and start moving, push the child slightly forward. This is a new experience for the child.

6   Massage.

WEEK 3

1   The structured conversation this week looks like this:

> anan
>
> enen
>
> inin
>
> onon
>
> anin
>
> anon

Vary the length of the sound sequences and the vowel that is being stressed.

2   Carry on with the imitation activities from weeks one and two. Here is an additional movement to stimulate in the same manner as during week one:

> The gesture 'Good!'

Remember **always** to use the Good gesture when you want to praise the child, for example every time an activity is completed, whether or not the child needed support when carrying out the activity.

3   The 'hide' and 'take and give' games may be varied by dropping the objects onto a table or on the floor in front of the child.

4   A new finger rhyme:

> Five fat sausages frying in the pan (hold up fingers)
>
> one goes pop another goes bang (pop cheek/clap hands for pop and bang)
>
> four fat sausages frying etc.

5   It may be useful if you are able to put up a baby bouncer in your house, for example in a doorway. The baby bouncer will give your child a lot of new experiences through the different movements that the baby bouncer makes. Please, seek advice from your Physiotherapist.

WEEK 4

1   The structured conversation this week looks like this:

> avaba
> avabo
> avabi
> adana
> adano
> adani

Vary the length of the sound sequences.

2   This week's imitation of gesture is the gesture for 'ball'.
    The child should be very familiar with a ball, that is, the child should know how it feels to touch a ball, that the ball rolls, that there are both large and small balls and so forth.

Remember, the goal is **not** for the child to use the sign ball, only to be able to imitate the movement.

A third person is needed.

- The child is sitting on your lap. Put a ball in the child's hands.

- The third person is sitting opposite the child with a ball in his/her hands and moves the ball up and down several times.

- Help the child to imitate this activity.

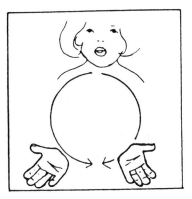

- The child and you plus the third person all make the sign for ball at the same time.

The following gestures and signs are used by you and all other family members all the time:

> look
> take
> give me
> come up
> hello, bye bye
> good
> ball

Every small attempt by the child to imitate anything that looks vaguely like these gestures should be interpreted as proper gestures by all family members. The child's early attempts to make specific gestures will be seen as meaningful communication and the child should be rewarded appropriately, for example by being lifted up as soon as you think the child has attempted to make the gesture for 'pick me up'.

3   The activity is carried out in the same way as during weeks 1 and 3.

4   Add more pages to the pointing book.

5   Carry out the activity in the same way as last week.

6   Massage.

There are various kinds of so-called activity toys which may start to have appeal for your child. The child is doing something (e.g. pressing a button) and something happens immediately (e.g. a bell rings).

If you are handy you can easily make one – for example, a battery operated bell. There are plenty of activity toys in toy shops.

WEEK 1

1   The structured conversation this week looks like this:

    Day 1: bob, bobodo

    Day 2: yoy, yoyowo

    Day 3: mom, momobo

    Day 4: non, nonodo

    Day 5: lol, loloyo

Vary the length of the sequences as well as the stress. Try to focus this activity towards gradually making the child sound more like you.

2   From now on the imitation of movements is focused on signing to a greater extent. However the child is not expected to start using signs for another few months.

    The purpose of the sign imitation is to help the child to feel how physically to make signs. The child's understanding of the signs will gradually increase by experiencing the signs in natural situations over a long period of time.

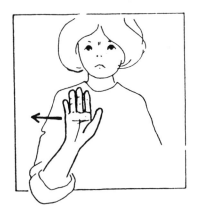

To learn words (spoken or signed) the child needs not only to **see** and **hear** but also to a high degree **feel**. This is the reason why the these imitation activities are important.

The sign imitation this week is the sign 'no'.

This sign should **always** be used when something is forbidden, dangerous or wrong. As before, a third person needs to assist you.

- Sit with the child on your lap.

- The third person is sitting opposite you and says 'Do this' (signing 'no'). The phrase 'Do this' should be used as a signal in all future sign imitation activities. The no-sign is repeated several times.

- Hold the child's hand and the sign is made simultaneously by the child and the third person.

3   The 'take and give' game is probably something you do quite often now. Add the sign 'Thank you' to the game. This marks the end of the play sequence.

- Say and sign 'Take...' while holding a toy in front of the child. Do not hold the toy too close to the child. The child has to lean forward to reach the toy.

- The child is exploring...

- Say and sign 'Give me...'. When the child has given you the toy say and sign 'Thank you'.

- This is the end of the activity and the toy is being put away.

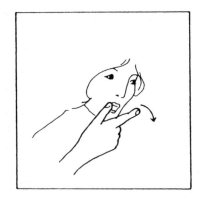

4   Continue to stimulate the child's hands and fingers in as many ways as you can think of.

   The child can tear out and crinkle the pages of an old telephone directory. This makes a lot of noise and the child has to use his/her hands and fingers. An old newspaper can also be used.

5   Massage and name the child's body parts.

WEEK 2

1   'Bombard' the child with the following sequence this week:

   Day 1: pap, papaba

   Day 2: pep, pepeme

   Day 3: pop, popowo

   Day 4: pip, pipibi

   Day 5: pup, pupuyu

   Is the child perhaps starting to copy one or two sounds?

2   The sign imitation this week is the sign for 'sleep'.

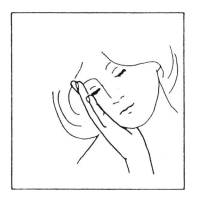

Remember that words in small children's vocabulary have a broader and more general meaning compared to the meaning of words for adults. It is useful to use the sign in suitable situations and not only in situations when the adult would say the word.

Use the sign 'sleep' in situations where adults would say

> sleep
>
> lie down
>
> tired
>
> bed
>
> night
>
> ...
>
> ...

The exact meaning of the words and the signs will gradually develop over the years.

3   Make the 'take and give' game more complex:

Put the toy on the table in front of the child instead of holding the toy. Point to the toy on the table in front of the child and say/sign

- 'Take...'

- When the child has finished exploring, say/sign 'Give me...'

- Say/sign 'Thank you' when you receive the toy.

4   Encourage the child to pick up small objects. Sit opposite the child. Give the child small objects (e.g. rice crispies) in the way shown in

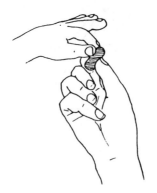

the illustration. This is one way of stopping the child trying to grasp objects while having the fingers flexed into the palm of the hand.

Explore the small objects together.

5   Massage.

WEEK 3

1   'Bombard' the child with the following sequence this week:

Day 1: gag, gagada

Day 2: geg, gegebe

Day 3: gog, gogobo

Day 4: gig, gigiyi

Day 5: gug, gugulu

Remember to play with the stress and the length of the sequences.

2   The sign imitation this week is the sign 'eat'

Think about what the sign 'eat' could mean to a small child. Think about the situations where eating takes place – it is even possible that a childminder could be included in the meaning of the sign, if the childminder's feeding of the child is a nice and positive experience for the child.

Use the sign in situations where you think it is suitable for your child.

Carry out the imitation activity in the same manner as before.

3   The 'take and give' game is made more complex by putting down two objects on the table, but the child is only asked to pick up one of the two objects. Ask the child to pick up the object you are pointing at.

If the child picks up the wrong object, use the sign 'no' at the same time as you take the object away. Only one item is then left on the table and you start again by asking the child to pick up the object...

Or instead of removing the 'wrong' item take the child's hand and together pick up the 'correct' object.

4   The activity continues in the same manner as during week 1 and 3.

5   Massage.

6   A lot of learning takes place in everyday routine activities. Learning to recognise a room is an important step in the learning process. Start using the following **daily** routine. This is only a suggestion. Your own routine can be:

The 'Good morning' walk: Put the child on your arm each morning and walk around saying 'Good morning' to all the items which are always kept in the nursery, that is, do not say 'Good morning' but simply name each item to which you point for example window, light, bed... The 'Good evening' walk can take place in another room for example the kitchen: cooker, fridge, sink, light. Carry out this type of activity in all other rooms as well.

Take care to point out the items in the same order every day, at least in the beginning. The child's expectation for what is coming next will grow – and what you say is a reward for the child's guesses.

Structured routines of this kind may help the child to think ahead.

WEEK 4

1   From now on no more structured conversations will be suggested.
    Continue to talk to your child in this way, but let the child choose the sounds to a greater extent.
    However, it is still useful to vary the stress and the length of the sequences.

2   The imitation this week is not a sign but more of a play movement.
    The child is going to imitate a third person who is moving a toy car back and forth over the table.
    Put your hand on top of the child's hand and move another toy car across the table at the same time as the third person.

3   The 'take and give' game is continued. Encourage the child to make the 'give me' gesture before he/she receives the object.
    If the child does not spontaneously reach out his/her hand with the palm up, take the child's hand and make the gesture together. Put the object in the child's hand immediately afterwards.

4   For this activity you will need, for example, two saucepan lids or two toy bricks.

    Help the child as much as he/she needs in this activity. Initially, you may need to have the child on your lap, holding your hands on top of the child's hands.
    Grasp and hold on to the objects together and make the necessary movements (see illustration).

5   Massage.

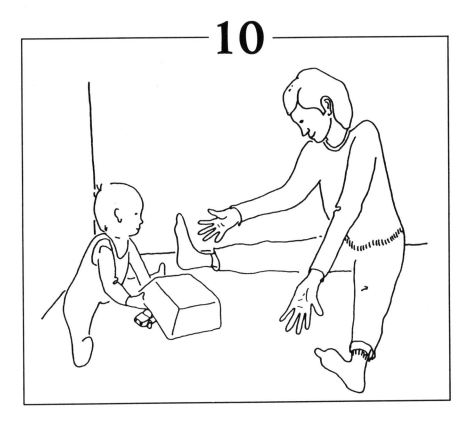

WEEK 1

1 Work consistently on a daily basis to encourage the child to imitate hand movements.

The sign imitation this week is the sign 'gone'. The aim of the activity is for the child to feel the physical movement, not to learn the concept.

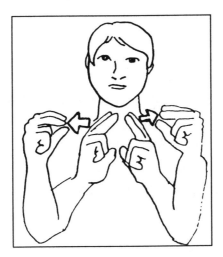

You need someone to help you.

- Sit down with the child on your lap.

- The third person sits opposite the child and says: 'Do this. Gone'. The 'gone' sign is repeated several times.

- Hold the child's hands while the sign is made simultaneously by all of you.

- Repeat the sign several times while giving the child less guidance, but always enough so the child is making the sign.

Every little attempt to imitate spontaneously should be much praised.

2   A doll and a hankie is needed for this hiding game. Try the following:

- The child is sitting opposite you.

- Hold the doll in front of the child while saying and singing: 'Look, a doll'.

- Put the doll in the child's hands. Cover the doll with the hankie.

- Say and sign: 'Gone'. Remember to use facial expressions and gestures as well.

- If the child does not remove the hankie, help the child to remove it.

- Say and sign: 'Peekaboo' (sign: look).

Repeat: Cover – remove – cover – remove...
          'gone' – 'look' – 'gone' – 'look'...

3   You will be provoking the child slightly during this activity.

Material: One of the child's favourite toys. (Use the same toy every day during the week.) A tea towel.
   Try the following:

- Start playing with the toy. Make sure the child is interested.

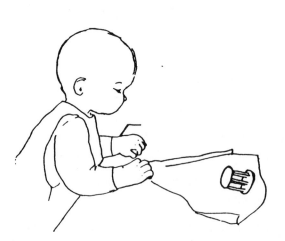

- When the child is paying attention, take the toy away from the child and put it slightly out of reach on the towel.

- One end of the towel is positioned near or underneath the child's hands.

- If the child does not pull the towel spontaneously to reach the toy, then help the child to do this. Put your hands on top of the child's hands and together pull the towel and pick up the toy.

Repeat this activity in exactly the same manner using the same objects until the child starts to understand what to do.

4   Encourage the child to participate in the following song which stimulates body awareness.
     Use the same tune each time you sing the song. Help the child to carry out the movements.

     Clap, clap your hands   *Clap your hands to the tune*
     Clap, clap your hands
     Clap, clap, clap

A new finger rhyme this week:

     Tom Thumbkin,
     Willie Wilkin,
     Long Daniel,
     Betty Bodkin,
     And Little Jack-a-Dandy

5   Another daily routine to be introduced:
     Give the child a small starter at meal times containing small bits of something which encourages chewing. The child is encouraged to pick up and chew while you are preparing the rest of the meal. Do not use soft bread or buns which may easily get stuck to the child's palate.

WEEK 2

1   The sign imitation this week is the sign 'car' plus the sound of a car.
     Work on the imitation in the same manner as before. Remember to sound like a car.
     Take all opportunities to make the sign 'car' with the child's hands – when you are playing with cars, while travelling by car and when you see a car, and so on. Use the sign imitation technique.

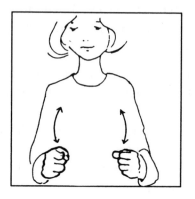

Remember: The child has to **make** (that is, sign or say) the word many times before he/she knows it. Therefore, do not expect the child to make the sign spontaneously.

2   Carry out the hiding game in the same manner as last week, but use a car instead of a doll.

   Make the sign for 'gone' with the child's hands.

3   Carry out the activity in the same way as last week using a tea towel but with two or three new toys which the child likes. If you want to make the activity more difficult, put the toys further away from the child.

A new verse of the song about the body:

Stamp, stamp your feet   *Stamp your feet to the tune*
Stamp, stamp your feet
Stamp, stamp, stamp

5   The routine of giving the child a starter.
    Perhaps the child needs help to pick up the food? Hand the bits from underneath to the child.

WEEK 3

1   The sign imitation this week is the sign 'baby'. This sign is also used for 'doll'.

Use the same sign imitation technique which was used last week.

2   The hiding game is similar to last week. The only change to the activity is that the toys which are going to be hidden are placed in the child's lap instead of in his/her hands.

    Cover – remove – cover – remove.

3   Carry out the activity in the same way as last week. Remove the tea towel and use something different instead, for example a piece of paper. Use the piece of paper during the whole week.

4   A new verse of the song about the body:

Touch, touch your tummy   *Touching your tummy to the tune*
Touch, touch your tummy
Touch, touch, touch.

A toe-counting rhyme:

Wee Wiggie
Poke Piggie
Tom Whistle
John Gristle
and old BIG GOBBLE
gobble, gobble!

Start with the little toe and end up by seizing the big toe and pretending to gobble it up.

5   Continue with the starter.

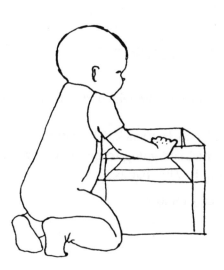

6   Find a box for the child to put things into. A fairly large, solid, wooden box is ideal. Encourage the child to pull him/herself up to look inside the box.

Fill the box with different objects, for example shoes, hats, books, empty plastic bottles.

Teach the child to pick up objects from the box and throw them on the floor.

WEEK 4

1   The sign imitation this week is the sign 'toothbrush' (clean your teeth).

Ideally, you hold a toothbrush each at the same time as you are making the sign.

Observe the child's own expressions in more detail. Pay extra attention to the child's eye gaze. Initially, the child is gazing without any particular purpose, but with time the gaze becomes more specific and conscious. The child starts to use his/her eyes to tell you that he/she wants something.

Try to interpret the child's expressions to give the child a positive response. React as if the child has said something. It is important to be aware of the fact that you are sometimes over-interpreting. Do not start to expect too much from the child.

2   This week's hiding game is carried out in the same way as last week.

Put the toys on a table instead of in the child's lap. Use various different toys and objects.

3   Carry out the activity in the same manner as last week.

Change the piece of paper to something different which will be used in the same way as the paper and the tea towel. A small pillow case or a scarf perhaps.

4   A new verse of the body song:

Touch, touch your nose	*Touching your nose to the tune*
Touch, touch your nose	
Touch, touch, touch	

Make up new verses of the song.

There are probably a number of games that your child likes:

- To be held up high near the ceiling.

- To fly up, down and round like an aeroplane.

Here is a rhyme to use when the child is sitting on your lap:

Father and Mother and Uncle John	*jog the child gently*
Went to market, one by one	
Father fell off!	*drop him/her to one side*
Mother fell off!	*drop him/her to the other side*
But Uncle John went on, and on, and on and on and on.	*now jog faster and faster*

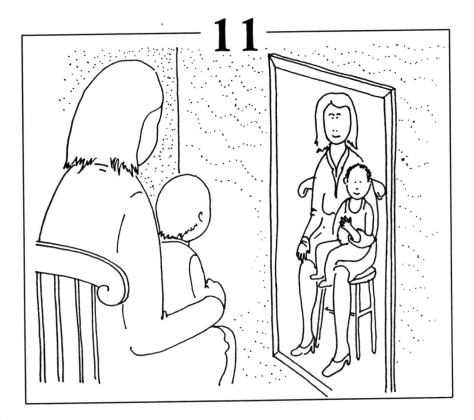

The stimulation you are giving your child is to a great extent aimed at encouraging the child's interest in trying out as many activities as possible.

Remember to make some situations a bit harder and more strenuous than others for the child.

When the child is sitting in the high chair by the table (without any food present on the table) perhaps you automatically put a toy in front of the child. Place the toy at a distance which will force the child to reach forward with his/her arms or perhaps reach sideways. Put the toy out of easy reach but make sure the child can see the toy.

The child who is standing with support may soon start to take steps sideways. Let the child stand by a sofa or a table of suitable height where the child can rest his/her arms on top of the table. Initially, it is a good idea if the child is able to stretch him/herself a bit. Gradually increase the expectations of sideways steps when the child masters the technique.

When the child is sitting on the floor, put some objects out of the child's reach. Let the child stretch with his/her arms and trunk to reach some objects, but make sure you put the favourite toy at a distance where the child has to move him/herself across the floor to reach.

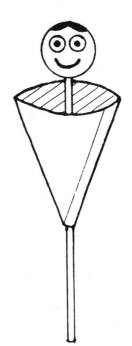

All sorts of peekaboo games are useful. A simple peekaboo doll can be made out of a cone of paper with a ball on a stick inside.

WEEK 1

1   The sign imitation this week is the sign **'Mummy'**.

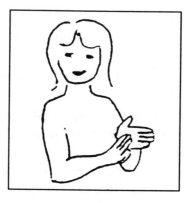

Use the same routine as before:

- Sit with the child on your lap.

- Your 'helper sits opposite the child and says the signal phrase: 'Do this: Mummy.' The sign for 'Mummy' is repeated several times.

- Hold the child's hands and make the sign for 'Mummy' at the same time as the helper.

- The sign for 'Mummy' is of course used by all the family members from now on.

2   You need two new toys for this activity. The toys should look very different from each other. Mechanical toys or sound making toys are suitable.

The two toys are to be called Beebie and Bibbie. If you find it strange to call, for example, a bird 'Bibbie', remember that this is the bird's name and strange-sounding names are not unusual!

The purpose of this activity is to stimulate the child's ability to differentiate important aspects of sound in speech.

This week you are working on the name

Beebie

where the first syllable is long and stressed and the second syllable is short and without stress.

Play all sorts of games with Beebie – give and take, hiding, peekaboo, jump on the child's tummy, and so on. Improvise but make sure the child is 'bombarded', 100 times a day if you want, with the name and the toy Beebie. This should make the child associate the name with the toy. Work on sign imitation as well since it is important for the child to **make** the name.

Imitation of hand movements are easier to make than speech imitation is for the child. Since you cannot help the child with the sound imitation but can help it with imitation of a gesture, combine the word Beebie with some sort of gesture (e.g. right hand with palm down, make a horizontal line in front of the chest). The gesture you choose to make will become the sign for the toy.

3   Provoke the child a bit this week. All toys that are used in the activity should have a ribbon or a string attached.

Try the following:

• Start playing with the child using one of the toys.

- When the child is playing with the toy – remove the toy.

- Place the toy out of the child's reach. Put the string or the ribbon in or near the child's hand.

- If the child does not spontaneously pull the string to reach the toy – help the child to do this.

4   **Goal:** For the child to pick objects out of a box.

- Place one or two objects of the same sort in front of you on the table or the floor.

- Place a box near the child.

- Put one object at a time in the box while the child is paying attention to what you are doing. Make comments about what you are doing: 'Now I'm putting…in the box.'

- When the objects have been placed in the box, push it closer to the child. Play the old 'Give me' game in exactly the same way as you have done previously.

- Help the child if necessary.

Place the box in different positions in relation to the child – straight in front of and to one side or slightly raised (on a big book).

WEEK 2

1 The sign imitation this week is the sign **'Daddy'**.

Work in exactly the same way as last week.

2 Continue the activity from week 1.

3 Continue the activity from week 1.

4 The activity is carried out in the same way as during week 1, but use several items of the same sort.

Vary the objects **but** at each individual training session use only objects of the same sort.

WEEK 3

1 The sign imitation this week is the sign **'light (lamp)'**.

This sign is not easy to imitate correctly. Focus on the movement and the position of the hand. Do not bother too much about what the child is doing with his/her fingers.

Many children of this age seem to be fascinated by 'Look at the light' or 'point at the light' games. Play these games on a regular basis with your child and the sign for light will be used a lot. Help your child to look at and point to the light if necessary.

2   During this week you should teach the child to associate a toy with the name

Bibbie

where both syllables are short and have equal stress (like the stress of the name Anna).

Work in the manner that suits you and which will give the child maximum repetition. Do not forget the imitation and that you need to find a simple movement (e.g. right hand with palm down, pat down twice) which will become the sign for the toy.

3   This activity is carried out in almost the same manner as last week.

The child sits in the high chair and the toy is strapped to the 'arm' of the chair. Instead of putting the toy just out of reach on a horizontal surface, the child now has to pull the toy up, moving the toy vertically. The string should be **short**. Help the child if necessary.

4   The game using a box is changed this week in one important way.

You have four objects of the same sort plus one other object (e.g. four bricks plus one shoe).

The objects are already in the box when you start the activity. Ask the child to give you the objects. If there are bricks in the box, keep a small number of bricks in a pile next to you as well.

- The child gives you a brick. Put it next to you on the pile.

- The child gives you another brick. Put it in the same place.

- The child gives you the shoe. React with obvious surprise using clear body language while you say/sign 'No, no'.

- Take the shoe, point to the bricks and say 'No' again. Then put the shoe behind your back or somewhere where the child cannot see it.

- Ask for another brick and continue until the box is empty.

Repeat the activity as long as the child is paying attention.

WEEK 4

1   The sign imitation this week is the sign **'flower'**.

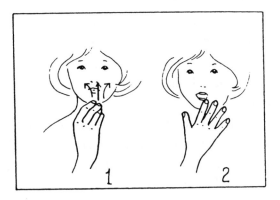

It is difficult to imitate the sign for flower correctly. Focus the imitation on making the child move his/her hands towards his/her nose while making a 'sniffing' sound.

The 'smell the flower' game is a game which a lot of children of this age are interested in. Play this game often.

The following 20 signs/gestures are always used by you and the other family members when you talk to the child:

look, take, give me, come, up, hello/bye bye, good, ball, no, thank you, sleep, eat, gone, car, baby(doll), toothbrush, Mummy, Daddy, light/lamp, flower.

2   Continue this activity the same way as last week. Towards the end of this week you will be using both toys – Beebie and Bibbie. Play 'give and take'.

- Hold up Beebie and say/sign 'Take Beebie'.

- Hold up Bibbie close to the child's other hand and say/sign 'Take Bibbie'.

- The child should now hold Beebie in one hand and Bibbie in the other hand.

- Point to one of the two toys and say its name and then point to the other toy and say its name.

- Then say/sign 'Give me Beebie'.

- If the child gives you the wrong toy, put your hand underneath the Beebie-hand and repeat; 'Give me Beebie' at the same time as you push the right hand lightly.

- When you have been given Beebie, ask for Bibbie in the same way.

If you try this activity without signs then the activity gives you the possibility to check that the child is hearing the difference between Bibbie and Beebie. You will also see if the child is associating the name with the right toy.

3   The activities using tea towels and strings are trying to develop the understanding that some objects can be used as tools to reach certain goals, for example to get hold of an object out of direct reach.

Continue with this type of activity. Make sure there are no valuable items on top of tablecloths. Examples of useful toys:

- Jumping jack. Moving arms and legs when someone pulls the string.
- Musical boxes. Only playing a tune when the string or handle has been pulled.
-

4   Continue with the activities from last week. Is it difficult to think of objects of the same sort?

Here are a few examples:

Four teaspoons plus a book
Four toothbrushes plus a doll
Four dolls' cups plus a hat

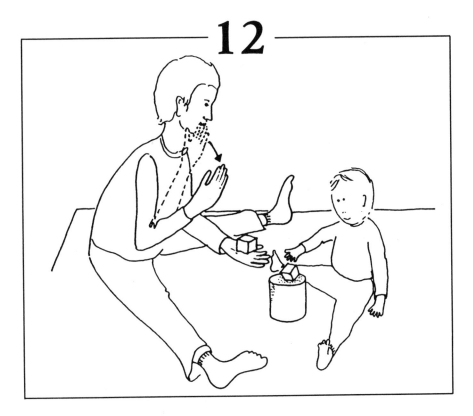

WEEK 1

1   From now on, try to sit in front of a mirror when you work on any sign imitation activity.

The sign imitation this week is the sign **'I'**.

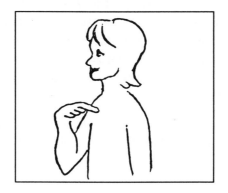

The sign 'I' is difficult to teach since who 'I' refers to changes depending on who is talking. I suggest that the sign I is used only instead of the child's name and the sign is made towards the child's chest. That is, when you talk to the child, say the child's name and simultaneously tap his/her chest. Ask the child in front of the mirror 'Where is…(the child's name)?' – 'There is…(the child's name).' at the same time as you touch the child's chest with his/her index finger.

Try the following imitation activity:

- Sit with the child facing you.

- The third person sits in front of the child (but without obscuring the mirror) and says: 'Do this' and points to his/her own chest (without saying 'I').

- Take the child's hand and touch the child's chest with his/her index finger while repeating the child's name several times.

It is important to begin separating oneself as a person from the surrounding world as early as possible. Working on the sign 'I' is a help in learning this concept. However, it will take a long while before the sign will function as a sign for 'I'. The child needs many, many repetitions.

Other signs to introduce from an early stage can be the following:

1. Come, look, take, give me, ball, up, hello/bye bye, good.

2. No, thank you, sleep (use the same sign for lying down, tired, bed, night), gone, car, toothbrush, baby, teddy/doll, Mummy, Daddy, light/lamp, listen/hear, more/again. The gestures and signs that you choose to use should always be used by you and the other members of the family. It is important that you choose signs that are important features in your child's life. The list is only giving suggestions and should not be followed rigidly.

Remember to make the signs with the child's hands, preferably in front of the mirror. Also help the child to point by using the index finger.

2   For this activity two new toys are needed which will each be given a name. Mechanical or activity toys may be suitable – but **do not** choose dolls because they will be used later on.

The name to work on this week is 'Meem' with a long and strong 'eee'.

Play all sorts of games and improvise however you like as long as the child is able to hear the name many times over.

The child should be encouraged to imitate the name Meem with a gesture (e.g. a circular movement made by rotating the right wrist – also a good activity for the wrist).

3   **Goal:** For the child to put a brick in a box.

Material: an empty box such as ice cream container (collect three boxes that look the same), a heap of bricks and a few other objects.

- Sit down with the box between you and the child. Say/sign 'Take the brick'. If the child does not spontaneously pick up the brick move the brick a bit closer to the child's hand and repeat the instruction.

- When the child holds the brick, say 'Put the brick in the box'.

- Give the child assistance and repeat many times over to make the child understand 'He/she should pick up the brick first, then put it in the box'.

- When you have given the child a few bricks which have been placed in the box, hand the child something completely different, for example a sock.

- It is important that you pretend to be very surprised. A sock is not a brick...

- Put away the sock and give the child another brick.

4   The child should be encouraged to point in all sorts of situations. He/she can point by using the whole hand, the thumb and finally the index finger. Help the child to point, for example during your daily walks around the house (the good morning and good evening routines). Hold the child's wrist and point towards the object you mention.

Picture books may start to be fun by now. There are many good picture books for sale. The pictures should not be too detailed and the pages should ideally only have one picture each.

The following pages can be coloured in, glued on cardboard and covered with plastic. It will then become a picture book with illustrations of objects the child is familiar with.

Point to the illustrations with the child's finger/hand.

WEEK 2

1   The sign imitation this week is the sign **'hat'**.

Work in front of a mirror. Start every imitation session by asking:
'Where is…(the child's name)?' – 'There is…(the child's name)' and
pointing to the child's chest.

Start playing in front of the mirror by putting hats on the child's
head – on and off a number of times using several different hats. Caps
with a peak are useful.

Remove the hats after a while and begin the sign imitation activity
in the same manner as last week.

2   This activity is carried out in the same manner as last week.
   Play the 'Give me-game' towards the end of the week with

   1 Meem and Beebie

   2 Meem and Bibbie

   3 Beebie and Bibbie

   - Hold Meem in front of the child and say/sign: 'Take Meem'.

   - Then hold Beebie in front of the child's other hand and
     say/sign: 'Take Beebie'.

   - The child is now holding (with or without your help) Meem
     in one hand and Beebie in the other hand. Point to the two
     toys one at a time and say their names.

- Reach out one of your hands towards Meem. Say/sign: 'Give me Meem'.

- If the child gives you Beebie, reach out your hand in an obvious way towards Meem and repeat the request at the same time as you touch the right hand.

- Request Beebie in the same manner.

- Complete this play activity by putting Meem and Beebie in a box.

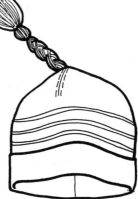

3   Carry out this activity in the same way as you did last week.

This week the box, for example a plastic ice-cream container, has the lid on. The lid has a big, round hole cut in it.

Continue to work with bricks, preferably round ones, but vary the odd object, which should not be put into the box. Remember to show your surprise in voice and body language every time the odd object turns up.

4   Continue in the same way as you did last week.

5   Do you roll balls to each other?

If not, you should start now. Perhaps the child needs a bit of help initially. Sit behind the child and roll the ball with the child's hands across the floor to a third person.

When the child starts to need less help in this game, make a joke by rolling the ball past the child. In this way you are encouraging the child to move as well.

WEEK 3

1   The sign imitation this week is the sign **'hear'** (listen).

Start the activity in the same way as last week by asking 'Where is...(the child's name)?' – 'There is...(the name) and

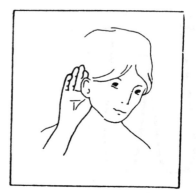

pointing to the child's chest.

Then continue with the imitation activity in the same manner as before.

2   This week a toy is named Mim with a short vowel sound. Work in the same way as during week 1.

(Suggested movement as a gesture for Mim: right hand touches left hand with both palms facing up).

3   Carry out the activity in the same way as you did last week.

The plastic lid used during last week is changed for another one, which has a slightly smaller hole cut out.

Don't forget to pretend to be surprised.

Save all the lids.

4   Carry out the activity in the same way as you did last week.

5   Carry out the activity in the same way as you did last week.

WEEK 4

1   The sign imitation this week is the sign **'more'** (another, one more time).

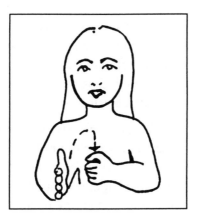

The sign will soon become very useful. Give the child many opportunities to make the sign with your help.

The following gestures/signs are always used by you and your family when you talk to the child:

look, take, give me, come, up, hello/bye bye, good, ball, no, thank you, sleep, eat, gone, car, baby, toothbrush, Mummy, Daddy, lamp, flower, I, hat, hear, more.

2   Continue to work with Meem and Mim, Beebie and Bibbie. Work in the same way as during week 2.

3   This activity should be carried out in the same manner as during week 1.

This week the box has a third lid, which has a suitable large hole for the bricks.

The child has three lids with different sized holes now. Give the child three boxes for these lids. Let the child use the boxes in unstructured play activities.

After a few weeks the activities can be carried on by adding another two lids, which have each got a different shape cut out. You should then together put bricks of different shapes into the right holes.

4   The activities are carried out in the same way as during week 2.

5   The activities are carried out in the same way as during week 2.

6   Give the child little presents. Hide objects in various sorts of paper. Use newspaper, wrapping paper and tissue paper. Different sorts of paper feel and crinkle in different ways.

You have now, over a period of time, been stimulating the child's ability to grip and handle objects.

- Soon there will be more intensive sign stimulation. To be able to carry out signs the child needs to have a certain hand control. The activities so far have focused on the child's control of the whole hand, the thumb as a separate part of the hand and to some extent the distinction between thumb, index finger and the whole hand.

Check if the child is capable of doing the following:

- Pick up objects.

- Grip small objects using thumb and index finger (not using a fully developed pincer grip but something similar).

- Pick up one object with right (left) hand and transfer the object to the other hand.

- Pick up one object with the right hand and another object with the left hand without letting the first object drop.

- Co-ordinate the movements of the hands for holding on to big objects.

- Co-ordinate the movements of the hands for clapping the hands together.

- Co-ordinate the movements of the hands for banging e.g. bricks together.

- Pointing using the index finger.

References

Åkerström, M. (1986) Motorisk stimulering av ett barn med Downs Syndrom 0–12 mån ålder. In publication number 26, Department of Phonetics, Umeå University, 34–44.

Alin-Åkerman, B. (1982) De första sju.åren. Natur och Kultur.

Alin and Nordberg, L. (1980) Griffiths' utvecklingsskalor I och II. Psykologiförlaget.

Bateman, B. and Wetherell, J. (1965) Psycholinguistic aspects of mental retardation. Mental Retardation 3, 8–13.

Bates, E., Camaioni, L. and Volterra, V. (1975) The acquisition of performatives prior to speech. Merrill-Palmer Quaterly 21, 205–226.

Bates, E., Benigni, L., Bretherton, I., Camaioni, L. and Volterra, V. (1977) From gesture to the first word: on cognitive and social prerequisites. In M. Lewis and L. Rosenblum (eds) Interaction, Conversation and the Development of Language. New York: Wiley and Sons.

Bates, E., Benigni, L., Bretherton, I., Camaioni, L. and Volterra, V. (1979) The Emergence of Symbols: Cognition and Communications in Infancy. New York: Academic Press.

Bloom, L. and Lahey, M. (1978) Language Development and Language Disorders. New York: John Wiley and Sons.

Bower, T. (1974) Development in Infancy. San Francisco: Freeman and Co.

Brazelton, T., Koslowski, B. and Main, M. (1974) The origins of reciprocity. In M. Lewis and L. Rosenblum (eds) The Effect of the Infant on its Caregiver. New York: Wiley.

Buckhalt, J., Rutherford, G. and Goldberg, K. (1978) Verbal and non-verbal interaction of mothers with their Down's syndrome and non-retarded infants. American Journal of Mental Disorder 82, 337–342.

Bullowa, M., Fidelholtz, J. and Kessler, A. (1976) Infant vocalization: communication before speech. In W. McCormack and S. Wurm (eds) Language and Man. Anthropological Issues. Mouton Publ.

Capute, A., Palmer, F., Shapiro, B., Watchtel, R. and Accardo, P. (1981) Early language development: clinical application of the language and auditory milestone scale. In R. Stark (ed) Language Behavior in Infancy and early Childhood. Alsevier North-Holland.

Cicchetti, D. and Scroufe, L. (1976) The relationship between effective and cognitive development in Down's syndrome infants. Child Development 47, 920–929.

Cicchetti, D. and Scroufe, L. (1978) An organizational view of affect: illustrations from the study of Down's Syndrome infants. In M. Lewis and L. Rosenblum (eds) The Development of Affect. New York.

Cohen, D. and Beckwith, L. (1979) Pre-term infant interaction with the caregiver in the first year of life and competence at age two. Child Development 50, 767–776.

Condon, W. (1979) Neonatal entrainment and enculturation. In M. Bullowa (ed) Before Speech: The Beginning of Interpersonal Interaction. Cambridge: University Press.

Condon, W. and Sander, L. (1974) Synchrony demonstrated between movements of the neonate and adult speech. *Child development 45*, 456–462.

Cross, T. (1977) Mothers' speech adjustments. The contributions of selected child listener variables. In C. Snow and C. Ferguson (eds) *Talking to Children: Language Input and Acquisition.* London.

Cunningham, C. (1982) *Down's syndrome, An Introduction for Parents.* Souvenir Press.

Cythryn, L. (1975) Studies of behavior in children with Down's syndrome. In E. Anthony (ed) *Explorations in Child Psychiatry.* New York.

Delack, J. (1975) Prosodic features of infant speech; the first year of life. Proceedings of the 8th international Congress of Phonetic Science.

Dunst, C. (1981) Social concomitants of cognitive mastery in Down's syndrome infants. *Infant Mental Health Journal 2*, 144–154.

Eilers, R., Wilson, W. and Moore, J. (1977) Development changes in speech discrimination in infants. *Journal of Speech and Hearing Research 20*, 766–780.

Ekström, K. and Johansson, I. (1986) SILD-testing av mongoloida barn. *Publication number 26*, 45–78. Department of Phonetics, Umeå University.

Emde, R., Katz, E. and Thrope, J. (1978) Emotional expression in infancy: Early deviations in Down's syndrome. In M. Lewis and L. Rosenblum (eds) *The Development of Affect.* New York.

Escalona, S. (1974) Development issues in the second year of life: Their implications for day care practice. *Psychosocial Press 31*, 28–33.

Freedle, R. and Lewis, M. (1977) Prelinguistic conversations. In M. Lewis and L. Rosenblum (eds) *Interaction, Conversation and the Development of Language.* New York.

Greenwald, C. and Leonard, L. (1979) Communicative and sensorimotor development of Down's syndrome children. *American Journal of Mental Deficiency 84*, 269–303.

Harding, C., and Golinkoff, R. (1979) The origins of intentional vocalizations in prelinguistic infants. *Child Development 50*, 33–40.

Johansson, I. (1983a) Tidig auditiv diskrimination hos barn med Downs syndrom. *Publication number 21*, 40–57. Department of Phonetics, Umeå University.

Johansson, I. (1983b) Early acquisition of prosodic and segmental cues: an experiment with infants with Down's syndrome. *Publication number 21*, 58–71. Department of Phonetics, Umeå University.

Johansson, I. (1983c) Jollerutveckling hos ett barn med Downs syndrom. *Publication number 21*, 17–39. Department of Phonetics, Umeå University.

Johansson, I. (1985) Mongoloida barns jollerutuecklings prövning av en analys modell. *Publication number 22*, 1–23. Department of Phonetics, Umeå University.

Kahn, L. (1975) Relationship of Piaget's sensorimotor period to language acquisition of profoundly retarded children. *American Journal of Mental Deficiency 79*, 640–643.

Kinney, W. (1979) The relationship of body image and perceptual motor performance of trainable mental retardated in a therapeutic recreation setting. *International Journal of Rehabilitation Research 2*, 215–224.

Kuhl, P. (1979) The perception of speech in early infancy. *Speech and Language.* Advances in Basic *Research and Practice vol 1* (ed Lass, N.). Academic Press.

Lindström, E. and Thurfjell, F. (1985) Aspekter av tidig kommunikation hos barn med Downs syndrom. *Publication number 24*, 1–48. Department of Phonetics, Umeå University.

Mead, G. (1934) (1967) *Mind, Self and Society from the standpoint of a Social Behaviorist.* Chicago: The University of Chicago Press.

Meltzoff, C. and Moore, M. (1977) Imitations of facial and manual gestures by human neonates. *Science 198*, 75–78.

Murphy, C. and Moore, M. (1977) Mothers, infants and pointing; a study of a gesture. In H. Schaffer (ed) *Studies of Mother–Infant Interaction.* New York: Academic Press.

Newport, E., Gleitman, L. and Gleitman, H. (1977) Mother I'd rather do it myself: some effects and non-effects of motherese. In C. Ferguson and C. Snow (eds) *Talking to Children. London University Press.*

Oller, D. (1978) Infant vocalization and the development of speech. Allied Health and Behavoral. *Sciences 1,* 523–549.

Piaget, J. (1952) The origins of intelligence in children. New York.

Rheingold, H., Bewirtz, J. and Ross, J. (1959) Social conditioning of vocalizations in the infants. *Journal of Comparative Psychology and Psychiatry 52,* 68–73.

Schaffer, H., Collis, G. and Parsons, G. (1977) Vocal interchange and visual regard in verbal and pre-verbal children. In H. Schaffer (ed) *Studies in Mother–Infant Interaction.* New York: Academic Press.

Sinclair, E. (1970) The transition from sensory-motor behavior to symbolic activity. *Interchange 1,* 119–126.

Sorenson, E. (1979) Early tactile communication and the pattering of human organization: a New Guinea case study. In M. Bullowa (ed) *Before Speech: the Beginnings of Interpersonal Communication.* Cambridge University Press.

Snyder, L. (1978) Communicative and cognitive abilities and disabilities in the sensori-motor period. *Merrill-Palmer Quaterly 24,* 161–188.

Stark, R. (1980) Stages of speech development in the first year of life. Child phonology vol 1 (eds Yeni-Konshian, G., Kavanagh, J. and Ferguson, C.) 73–92.

Steckol, K. and Leonard, L. (1981) Sensori-motor development and the use of prelinguistic performatives. *Journal of Speech and Hearing Research,* 262–268.

Stern, D. (1974) Mother and Infant at play: the dyadic interaction involving facial, vocal and gazw behaviors. In M. Lewis and L. Rosenbury (eds) *The Effect of the Infant on its Caregiver.* New York: Wiley.

Stern, D., Jaffe, J., Beebe, B. and Bennett, S. (1975) Vocalizing in unison and in alternation: Two modes of communication within the mother–infant dyad. In D. Aronson and R. Reiberg (eds) *Developmental Psycholinguistics and Communication Disorder.* Ammals of the New York Academy of Sciences 263.

Thomas, E.E. (1994) Early language intervention in children with Down's syndrome. Primary Care Development Fund project 77/89. Eastbourne and County Healthcare, Speech and Language Therapy Services, Sturton Place, Station Road, Hailsham, E. Sussex.

Trevarthen, C. (1979) Communication and co-operation in early infancy: a description of primary intersubjectivity. In M, Bullowa (ed) *Before Speech: The Beginning of Communication.*